Help!
My Loved One Is in Prison

Help! My Loved One Is in Prison

Practical Steps to Take
If Your Friend or Loved One
is Currently or Formerly
Incarcerated

Louis N. Jones
Laverne Brewster

Washington, D.C.

Conquest Books
A division of ConquestHouse, Inc.
PO Box 73873
Washington, DC 20056-3873

Copyright 2001, 2005 by ConquestHouse, Inc. All rights reserved.

Printed in the United States of America

ISBN: 0-9656625-1-9

Scripture quotations ending with the abbreviation (NASB) taken from the New American Standard Bible, copyrighted 1960, 1962, 1963, 1968, 1971, 1972, 1973, 1975, 1977, by the Lockman Foundation. Used by permission.

Scripture quotations ending with the abbreviation (NIV) excerpted from *Compton's Interactive Bible NIV*. Copyright (c) 1994, 1995, 1996 SoftKey Multimedia Inc. All Rights Reserved

---

CONTENTS

INTRODUCTION	VII
THE PROBLEM ON THE OUTSIDE	1
DEFINITION OF A LOVED ONE	3
PREPARE YOURSELF	5
TYPES OF SUPPORT	13
HOW TO HELP WHILE HE IS STILL IN PRISON	17
ADDRESSING OTHER VITAL NEEDS	31
HOW FAR DO I GO?	37

YOUR LOVED ONE'S RELEASE OPTIONS	47
MENTORING	55
GETTING A GOOD CHRISTIAN SUPPORT BASE	65
HOUSING	69
ASSISTANCE WITH EMPLOYMENT	83
ISSUES CONCERNING WOMEN EX-OFFENDERS	103
APPENDIX	111
NATIONAL AGENCIES THAT MAY BE OF ASSISTANCE TO THOSE HELPING INMATES AND EX-OFFENDERS	111
REFERENCES	114

Introduction

Over the past several years, I have received letters and emails from people all over the country who have loved ones in prison and are seeking assistance for them. Many of these letters testify to the lack of available services and assistance for ex-offenders. These letters are from friends, parents, sons, daughters, spouses, siblings, girlfriends, and boyfriends, all of whom have loved ones in prison and don't know how to help them. This book is written for all these people.

Often, the most important elements of the ex-offender's successful re-entry into society are the people who love him and care for him and stand around him. These people can be more effective than any social service program or organization. As the director and founder of a non-profit organization that works with ex-offenders, I have quickly realized that my organization cannot help every person who comes to me. While it is a fact of life, it is nonetheless unfortunate. Writing this book can help empower these parents, these siblings, these spouses, and other loved ones with information and advice that will aid them in helping their loved ones, and that is a great joy to me. That this book could help some girlfriend or boyfriend or son or daughter help their loved ones get their lives together and stay out of prison is my goal. I pray that this book helps you to achieve that goal.

Preparing your loved one at least six months ahead of release is essential. In fact, it would be best to begin preparation long before any parole or probation hearing, so that an adequate plan can be presented to the authorities as evidence that he has support in the community.

Let me make one thing clear. The intent of this book is not to help your friend or loved one get out of prison just for the sake of getting out. This book is intended to help those who are serious about turning their lives around and want to do whatever it takes to live a crime-free lifestyle and avoid a return to prison. Many people plan to get out but never plan for what they will do after they get out. Unfortunately, when it comes to planning for an inmate's release, many people feel the task ends once the inmate is out, and the prison gates shut behind him. But it is not over. The job is just beginning. Neglecting post-release planning may result in the inmate making a return trip to the inside of those prison gates.

Some of the ideas in this book will require you to do some legwork. That is the nature of the beast. Helping ex-offenders is not cushy work that can be done in an air-conditioned office in a few minutes a day. If you want to help an ex-offender, whether he is your loved one or a friend, helping will be time-consuming. You will have to scour your community for resources, which are often scarce. If you are lucky and blessed enough to find an agency that provides a full range of services so that you will not have to do much, you will still have to do some legwork to find that agency. There aren't many of them; hundreds more are needed.

You will notice in this book that I frequently use the male pronouns "he" or "him" or "his" when referring to ex-offenders. I have written this way merely to avoid the awkward use of "he or she" or "him or her" in every other sentence. Because the majority of ex-offenders in America are male, (although the numbers of female inmates are increasing), I chose to use masculine pronouns in my discussions. However, in no way does this mean that this book is directed at only male ex-offenders. Everything in this manual applies to women as well.

There is much in this book that will be helpful to persons who have loved ones in prison, regardless of their religion. However, everything in this book has been written to adhere to sound Biblical principles. I do not quote the Bible profusely in this book because I do not intend for it to be used as a Bible study. It is, simply, a hands-on guide for people who desire to help their incarcerated loved ones. But I took great pains to make sure that nothing in this book is contrary to Christian belief.

CHAPTER ONE

The Problem on the Outside

Your loved one or friend is about to be released. Your loved one or friend may have been guilty of the crime or may have been falsely accused. It doesn't really matter. What matters is that the inmate is being released with a stamp on his or her forehead. The stamp reads, "I AM A FORMER INMATE. I COMMITTED A CRIME. I AM NOT TO BE TRUSTED." This is what many people see when they encounter an ex-offender. It doesn't matter if the person was guilty or innocent of the crime. Most people trust their judicial system enough to believe that if a person spent a significant period of time locked up, there is a good chance the person did the crime, no matter what he might claim. So, the ex-offender will have to live with this stamp on his forehead, whether he committed the crime or not.

That is the problem. Past criminal behavior has become the de facto standard for whether or not a person is to be trusted. Many job applications ask the question, "Have you ever been convicted of a crime?" Once you are convicted, you are branded. No one wants to hire you. No one wants to give you a place to live, because they cannot trust you around their belongings and their children. In some states you are not even allowed to vote or get a government grant to start a business.

Yet despite this grim outlook, there is hope. Ex-offenders all over the country are being hired in productive jobs. They are becoming excellent role models, fathers, and mothers to their children. They are becoming responsible citizens of the community. Is it possible to make it despite the grim outlook I have painted in the previous paragraph? YES, IT IS. All an ex-offender needs is determination and willingness to do whatever it takes to succeed and follow the suggestions offered in this book.

CHAPTER TWO

Definition of a Loved One

Since this book is targeted to your "loved ones" who are in prison, nearly released, or already released, I feel the need to define the term. A "loved one", as referred to in this book, is any inmate or ex-offender whom you are in a romantic, brotherly, or spiritual relationship with. A loved one is a person whose faults you can look beyond to see the potential. A loved one is a person for whom you desire to do all you can do to help. A loved one is a person for whom you are willing to give your money, time, and attention, not for your personal gain but for his sake.

As such, this book is directed not only at family or close friends of inmates but also to pastors, social service providers, chaplains, and any others who have people in prison they love and desire to see reach their full potential.

CHAPTER THREE

Prepare Yourself
(Read This if You Read Nothing Else)

Most of the advice and suggestions you will read in these pages will focus on your efforts to help that special loved one who is in prison or who is newly released. But this section will focus entirely on *you*. Since you have a loved one in prison, and presumably this person has a love for you as well, you are in a good position to provide assistance to this individual. However, it is crucial to acknowledge that you may not be the best person or the only person to help him.

I am not trying to discourage you from helping your loved one. But the purpose of this section is to help you to examine yourself and determine whether you are ready, willing, and able to take on the task of helping a loved one affected by the criminal justice system. Loving this person does not necessarily qualify you to help this person with every need. Since the ex-offender's freedom is at stake, it is better to recognize that you cannot do the job entirely by yourself and need to get help, rather than try to take it all on yourself and do more harm than good.

Helping an ex-offender takes time, money, skill, and energy. If you are limited in any of these areas, there is only so much you can do. I have met parents of inmates who have committed themselves to helping their sons and daughters in prison, yet the parents were so overwhelmed with their own concerns and issues that they couldn't see clear to help their children. I am not saying you should not help in those circumstances, but that you should recognize your limitations and get help wherever possible.

I would recommend that you read this book in its entirety and discover all it takes to help an ex-offender. Then, after reading, you should perform a self-inventory and determine what areas you can provide help with and what areas you cannot. Get help for those areas you cannot. Never promise an ex-offender more than you can deliver.

As an example of never promising more than you can deliver and getting help when you need it, I think about an act of love I will never forget, and indeed, think about to this day. I grew up in an immediate family that consisted almost entirely of females. I was the only male. My father did not live with the family, and I saw him once or twice a year, mostly during holidays such as Christmas and the 4th of July, when he would invite the family over to his home for cookouts.

My mother, however, recognized something was needed in my life. She saw this while I was in elementary school, and she knew she could not provide it herself (what a difference from today's super parents who believe they can do anything and everything for their children). So, she had conversations with the administrators in my school and tried to arrange for me to be in as many classes per day that were taught by male teachers. Why? Because she wanted me to have a male mentor. Since my family was comprised of mostly females, she wanted a positive male influence to spend time with me and guide me into real manhood. She knew she could not get that kind of commitment from the other males in my extended family. She even signed me up for the *Big Brothers Big Sisters* program, which puts positive mentors into the lives of children. This, in my opinion, was love at its finest. She recognized there was a dimension that she could not provide, and she did not agonize over it. She sought help. That decision made me a much better person today.

What are your limitations? You need to quickly recognize those limitations and respond accordingly. If there is only *one* thing in this book that you can do effectively for your loved one, do not feel guilty or ineffective or useless. But whatever you can do, do it well. And get some help for the other areas that you cannot address.

<u>The ultimate help</u>
This is where the Christian bias in this book begins to show. And I do not apologize for it, because I would be remiss not to mention the one source of help that is greater than all others. And that help comes from God.

I have come to recognize in my Christian life that humankind would be a dismal failure if left to their own devices. All of the best minds and strongest bodies in the world cannot compensate for the blessings that God makes available to us. The world is standing today due to the blessings of God. If it were not for Him, we would have destroyed this earth a long time ago.

No matter how smart we are, or how strong we are, or how much money, influence, or power we have, we are still very limited. The power of the world is no match for the power of God. Jeremiah 10:12 reminds us that "God made the earth by his power; he founded the world by his wisdom and stretched out the heavens by his understanding ." No one on earth can sanely claim to have as much power to create the earth and heavens. The power of humanity pales in comparison to the power of God.

But the good news is that God makes His power available to those who believe in Him. The great praise to God at the end of the book of Jude reads, "to the only God our Savior be glory, majesty, power and authority, through Jesus Christ our Lord, before all ages, now and forevermore." God makes His divine power available to us by grace through faith in Jesus Christ.

No one is meant to function without God's enabling power. To attempt to do so is futile and leads to frustration. There are many people and organizations that attempt to do social service without bringing God into the situation. Some of them seem to have great success at doing it. This leads one to draw the conclusion that God, or religion, or Christianity is not needed for social service—that it is strictly an act of human power.

I agree, to an extent. You do not need God explicitly to do social service. You do not need God to find housing for ex-offenders. God is not explicitly needed to get an ex-offender a job. People do it all the time without acknowledging God at all, and because of this, many of them have come to believe that God is not important or relevant in social service.

But I believe that God is relevant in all things. Even the successes that are achieved and experienced by those who do not know or acknowledge Him fall under the umbrella of the blessings of God. God's blessings are so bountiful, and His influence so widespread, that if He were to turn His back on the world for an hour, it would fall apart. He is so much in control that even evil people are manipulated by Him for His own purposes (Romans 9:17 makes this point). So, no one can say that God does not play a role in whatever happens in this world.

Social service seems to be effective without God. But to make it truly effective, the Lord must become a senior partner in the process. For no social service, no matter how well run, can change a man's heart. Only the power of God through the teaching of His word can do that. When you have in your hand social service skills and abilities, as well as God's life-changing power flowing through you, you can be a radical force for change in the life of your loved one. You will not only help to change his situation but also to change his heart. And with God's power flowing through you, you also have the power to withstand the following temptations to:

- give up on your loved one,
- become frustrated when things do not happen as quickly as they should,
- feel guilty if your efforts do not work,

- feel inadequate if you cannot do everything your loved one needs,
- become consumed with meeting his needs, without taking care of your own needs and responsibilities,
- become an enabler,
- assume his responsibilities as your own,
- avoid praying for him on a daily basis,
- avoid asking God for the blessings you need to support your loved one through his re-entry process.

How to get prepared
First of all, read through this book and get an idea of the types of needs and issues facing ex-offenders upon their release from prison. Next, take inventory of yourself and of your loved one. Determine the areas in which he is in need. Then determine which of those areas you can provide assistance in and which areas you cannot address without help. Find a quiet place, get down on your knees, and ask God for the enabling power to help your loved one. First, repent of any unrequited sin in your life and ask God to forgive you (this would be a good opportunity to forgive others who have wronged you, as well). Ask God to reveal to you the areas in which you can help. Ask God to bless you with the resources you need to move forward. Indicate your desire to help your loved one come to God's fullest potential. Indicate your desire to be used by God to make a powerful impact on the life of your loved one. And, pray for your loved one, pray that he will be receptive to your efforts and that the both of you will be blessed and kept from evil during the process.

If you are not a Christian, you can still follow the advice and suggestions in this book, and trust that they will work for your loved one. Many of them will. But the condition of your loved one's heart may cause him to destroy all of your efforts. For instance, when a man's heart is into selling drugs and making quick money, getting him a job where he labors 45 hours a week lifting heavy boxes for minimum wage seems like a good thing only on the surface. But it is like putting duct tape on a broken water pipe. It may hold for a moment, maybe longer than expected, but eventually, the tape will lose its grip and the pipe will burst.

Without God's power and presence in your own life, you will never know the peace, joy, and righteousness that come from living a life in accordance with God's will and desire for your life. You may have fleeting successes and notable achievements, but you will never know the peace and joy of God, which sustains those who are faithful and helps them to stand firm in the midst of any storm.

In caring for an ex-offender, you will unwittingly invite those storms. Are you fully prepared? If not, then you will want to call a pastor or minister in your area and have him or her lead you into salvation and into a relationship with Jesus Christ. This prayer can also be used to lead your loved one to Jesus Christ. If you do this earnestly and sincerely, Christ will come into your life and bestow upon you the peace, joy, happiness, and eternal power that can only be found in Him. Only then will you be truly prepared for the journey with your loved one.

CHAPTER FOUR

Types of Support

As you begin to support your loved one in his transition to society, you need to be aware that the support the ex-offender needs falls into the following categories:

Social
Spiritual
Family
Financial

Social
In order for an ex-offender to successfully transition into society, he must have a network of positive, caring friends and agencies that will provide a supportive community for him. One of your first responsibilities as a helper will be to find other friends to surround him during his transition.

As a minister to ex-offenders, I have quickly come to recognize that when an ex-offender is released from prison, Satan is at the door waiting. He would love nothing more than to get the ex-offender involved with the same friends and associates he was involved with before he went to prison. the devil will even try to convince the ex-offender that these are the only friends he can relate to. And while you should never force friends on your loved one, it is helpful for him to see that there are people around him who love him and care for him. It is helpful when it comes to choosing people to hang around, that he have a choice and does not have to fall back on the same negative friends and relationships.

Mentors are special friends who will be very helpful in his transition process. See the chapter titled *Mentoring* for more information.

Spiritual

Spiritual support involves not only getting the ex-offender into a church home but much more. It has been my experience that ex-offenders seem to have their greatest struggles when church is not in session. In addition to having a good Christian mentor in his life, there need to be people who will commit themselves to pray for the ex-offender, counsel him, and encourage him in his walk with Christ.

See the chapter titled *Getting a Good Christian Support Base* for a discussion of this topic.

Family

An ex-offender can have good friends in his life and may have a good Christian support base, but there can still be something missing. Any person, ex-offender or otherwise, can be surrounded by other people yet still feel lonely. He may feel like he has no one to talk to who will understand him or avoid condemning him. He may feel like there is no one he can trust.

If your loved one has supportive relatives, they should be encouraged to be especially supportive during this process. If he has no relatives, he can build a family out of his social and spiritual base. Eventually, if he continues to adhere to his social and spiritual base, he will come to love and trust the people in his life just as if they were his own blood.

Financial

Finances are the springboard from which all physical needs (food, shelter, clothing, etc.) are met. Therefore, getting the ex-offender a source of income is very important in the transition process. In fact, when it comes to ex-offender aftercare, income maintenance is usually the all-encompassing subject. While this is important, the social, spiritual, and family needs must be met in conjunction with the financial need.

CHAPTER FIVE

How to Help While He Is Still in Prison

If your loved one is still incarcerated, there are several things that you can do to ensure that his stay there is as smooth and trouble-free as possible. I should caution that most of the suggestions listed below are based on our experiences with some federal and state prisons and jails and do not necessarily reflect all prisons and jails. Nonetheless, following the suggestions below may help you get a step ahead in ensuring that your loved one is well-protected.

Stay informed
A lot of the hassle, trouble, confusion, and miscommunication that can happen when a loved one is incarcerated is simply the result of a lack of information. Therefore, one of the best things you can do for your loved one is to make sure that you are kept abreast of any and all information about the prison and the criminal justice system. Prisons change their policies all the time, often without letting anyone know. So, the more you know, the more you are able to help your loved one.

There are several people inside the prison you should get to know well—the warden, the case manager, and the chaplain. The warden is in charge of the prison. The case manager deals with prisoners' social and psychological issues and is usually the one who works with prisoners on a one-on-one basis to handle parole issues. The chaplain provides accommodations and services to meet the prisoners' religious needs. Get their numbers, call them, and ask them about prison policies and services (in some cases, it may be best to get this information from the Department of Corrections in your state or in the case of federal prisoners, from the Federal Bureau of Prisons). The following are some suggestions for things to ask about:

1) Visitation policies—Who can visit the inmates? When are visits allowed? What are the rules regarding visits?

2) Phone policies— Can the inmates receive calls at the prison, and if so, how? Are prisoners limited as to whom they can call? What are the costs of collect calls made from the prison?

3) Policies regarding the handling of inmate money and finances—What happens to money if it is sent to an inmate from a loved one? Is it used to pay off outstanding debts before the inmate gets it? Will his money be available for him once he leaves prison, and if so, where and when can he retrieve it? Will the inmate have to pay for his own personal effects in prison? What other expenses

is the inmate responsible for?

4) Mail policies — Can the inmate receive mail from anyone? If not, who can send mail to an inmate? Is the mail opened before the inmate gets it? How should mail to an inmate be addressed? What can be mailed to an inmate? What is an inmate allowed to mail?

5) Religious policies — Is the inmate allowed to attend religious services? If so, when? What other religious programs exist at the prison? Can a pastor or minister visit the inmate? Will the prison make accommodations for the inmate's practice of his faith?

6) Work and education — What employment opportunities are available for inmates at the prison? How can an inmate take advantage of them? Are there any educational programs, such as GED classes, college, or university courses leading to a degree, vocational courses, life skills seminars, etc.?

7) Disciplinary policies — What rules of conduct for inmates exist at the prison? What happens if an inmate breaks a rule? What procedures are in place to prevent inmate abuse and harsh discipline? Who is responsible for determining disciplinary action? How is the decision made?

8) Grievance policies — What procedure should the inmates follow if they have a

grievance against any prison staff member or official? Are there policies in place, and are the staff members trained to handle inmate grievances?

The following are other ways to keep yourself informed about prisons and their practices:

1) Find a prisoner advocacy group in your community and join them. One such group is CURE (Citizens United for Rehabilitation of Errants).

2) Find out which local newspapers cover the jurisdiction where the prison is located. Subscribe to the papers if at all possible.

3) Network with other people who have loved ones in the same prison. When you go to visit your loved one, talk with others in the waiting area. Ask about their experiences.

4) Find out which local government regulatory body or committee is responsible for overseeing prisons. Get on their mailing lists and plan to attend as many of their meetings as possible.

5) Most of all, ask your loved one. He is probably one of the best sources of information on the inside.

Keep in contact on a regular basis
Maintain regular and consistent contact between yourself and your loved one. Not only does this let your

loved one know that you are concerned for him and thinking about him, but it also lets you know that your loved one is alive and well. Perhaps you and your loved one can agree to contact each other, either by letter, phone, or your personal visit, at least once or twice a week. If you do not get a communication from your loved one once or twice a week as agreed, assume that something is up.

Also, if you are a family member of the inmate, studies have shown that regular contact between an inmate and his family can actually help reduce recidivism. In Washington, DC, most of our prisoners are shipped all around the country to federal, state, and private prisons, sometimes thousands of miles away. This is effectively destroying the family bond, as family members often have no means of transportation to get to the prison and visit with their loved ones.

Advocate tirelessly
One of the biggest needs an inmate has is for an advocate on the outside, someone he can trust. Prisons are not known for having trustworthy people (and I am not talking about just the inmates!) If you have a loved one in prison, and you are agreeing to help him, you are also his advocate. You should be willing to fight for him rather than let the prison system destroy him.

I've mentioned a prisoner advocacy group called CURE. I would strongly recommend that you contact their national office and find out if they have a chapter in your state. If so, join them. It only costs a few bucks per year. I know Pauline and Charlie Sullivan, who run the national CURE office. I am particularly impressed by their drive and commitment to the fight for the rights of prisoners. They have the audacity to believe that prisoners, regardless of what they have done, should be treated like human beings, not animals.

When you act as an advocate, you are not agreeing with or dismissing what the inmate has done. You are merely acting in his best interest, recognizing that he, like all of us, sometimes does the wrong thing. But he doesn't deserve to be treated like a dog because of it.

Realize the system is not perfect

I have no doubt that many people in the criminal justice system—judges, lawyers, police officers, parole and probation officers, corrections officers, wardens, etc.— are good, hardworking people who do their jobs with pride and dignity. But the correctional system, just like any other system, has a few bad eggs. You may encounter one of these people—someone who treats inmates as if they were lifeless pieces of paper on his desk. They may have absolutely no regard for the fact that their sloppy work will negatively affect someone for the rest of his life.

I have encountered this too many times to ignore this subject. I had a man walk out of prison homeless because a case manager failed to make a four-minute phone call to a transitional shelter to sign him up. In another case, a man stayed in prison up until his parole date, rather than spending six months in a halfway house as promised, because a case manager let his paperwork sit on her desk for weeks. Just recently, a parole officer accused one of my clients of using drugs (with no prior history of drug abuse) after a urinalysis indicated the presence of cocaine. The parole officer later confessed that my client's and another gentleman's urine samples got mixed up.

Mistakes, sloppy work, and uncaring attitudes can make your life and the life of your loved one more difficult. In some situations, there may not be a lot you can do about it. But you need to know that if your loved one accuses a prison staff member or official of wrongdoing, don't automatically write it off.

Prisoners often don't have anyone to believe in them. In prison, the guards, the prison staff, and the officials assume that if something goes wrong, you're guilty until proven innocent. Society has conditioned itself to believe that if an ex-offender is in dispute with anyone, the ex-offender is lying or is the guilty party. This is why it can be very difficult to prove wrongdoing or neglect on the part of prison officials. People automatically assume that the prison officials are right, and the prisoners, because they have committed crimes, are wrong.

If your loved one accuses any prison official or staff member of wrongdoing, then you need to use discretion as to how you will deal with it. In some situations, it is best not to confront anyone in the prison about these issues. This is particularly true if you or your loved one is concerned that raising the issue of a staff member's wrongdoing may result in retaliation against your loved one. (The staff member may not do it, but he or she can get prisoners to do it.) Prisons can be very dangerous and evil places, so this is common.

If there is a prisoner advocacy group in your community that fights for the rights of prisoners, you may want to let them know about these accusations. They can present these issues to prison officials in such a way that no particular inmate appears to have raised them. Oftentimes prison advocacy groups compile lists of problems and issues from prisoners and their loved ones and develop evidence of a systemic problem in the prison. In any event, keep records. If your loved one complains about a problem or situation in the prison, write it down. Get as many details as possible (keeping in mind that sometimes phones are monitored and letters are checked). Which brings me to the next suggestion . . .

Get an attorney
Since communication between an inmate and his lawyer is protected under attorney-client privilege, specific details about persons and accusations of wrongdoing should be shared with an attorney. By law, communication between attorneys and client-inmates is privileged and cannot be recorded or read unnecessarily. Mail sent between inmates and their attorneys should be sent following the prison's procedure for the handling of legal mail. (Note: Let your loved one know that merely marking an envelope "legal mail" does not necessarily mean that it will not be examined or opened. Legal mail may be protected only if it is handled in accordance with the prison's policies for handling such mail).

Many states and cities have attorneys who work with offenders. If your state has a public defender or legal aid office, you may be able to retain an attorney or get referrals from that office. There is also a directory titled *Legal Aid and Defender Offices in the US and Territories*. This book is listed in the Appendix.

Things you should not do
The following are suggestions of things that you definitely should not do when dealing with a loved one in prison:

Try to get him out before he is ready
Mothers love their sons. Wives love their husbands. Children love their parents. Boyfriends love their girlfriends. They do not want to see their loved ones locked up any more than the loved ones want to be there. They hate to see them suffer. Therefore, they may act instinctively to end that suffering and get their loved one out of prison anyway they can.

I realize how difficult it can be to follow this rule. But I also realize that not every person in prison is ready to be released to the streets. Incarceration, no matter how imperfect it is, serves a purpose. The purpose is to keep criminals off the streets until they have seen the error of their ways and have set about to change themselves. It is better to keep a person in prison if he is not ready for the outside world than to get him released before he is ready, only for him to go back out on the streets and do the same things he was doing before. In many cases, a mother's love has caused unrepentant criminals to be released on the streets to harm others, themselves, or society. What you must realize is that it is also an act of love to recognize when your loved one is not ready to be released to the streets and avoid doing anything to hasten his departure.

Be unnecessarily contentious with prison guards, staff, officials, or other related personnel
Nowhere is the skill of diplomacy better applied than in dealing with prison officials and staff. You are dealing

with people who have in their hands the medical care, security, education, comfort, and employment of your loved one. Therefore the last thing you should do is cause unnecessary friction between the staff and you.

Whenever I go to prisons, I am as nice to everyone as I can possibly be. I greet guards and staff. I treat them like the professionals they are. I respect the job they do. And I obey the rules of the facility. It doesn't matter whether I think they are corrupt or not. When I have someone in prison who I care about, I have to realize that these men and woman control my access to that loved one. Being contentious without reason makes you stick out like a sore thumb in the minds of prison staff and could affect your ability to visit the prison again.

Support any criminal wrongdoing
This should be glaringly obvious and does not need much explanation. No matter what your relationship is with the inmate, do not do anything that is criminal or could be construed as criminal activity. I often advise mentors, in dealing with inmates, to avoid running errands or passing messages back and forth, unless it is something that will help the ex-offender's development. Crafty inmates can use connections in the community to help them run illegal enterprises, and sometimes the hapless middlemen are none the wiser.

Mentoring the family: The mourning after
Helping an inmate in prison involves not only serving that inmate directly but also helping the inmate's family cope with the fragmentation of their family structure because of the loss of the inmate. This loss is due not to physical death but to separation from a loved one who is incarcerated in the prison system. No matter what

crime these individuals may have committed, there may be someone who is mourning their loss. There is a father or mother mourning the loss of a son or daughter. There is a son or daughter mourning the loss of a parent, and there is a sister or brother mourning the loss of a sibling. Because there are so many people affected by the mounting numbers of Americans being incarcerated, a serious problem for the structure of family life here in the United States has been created. Incarceration has created a void in the family. It is not only the physical loss that is felt; financial, emotional, and spiritual issues arise as well. Families often feel ostracized and abandoned by other family members, communities, and even the church. As a result, they often erect barriers to protect themselves from any further pain.

Often people who want to help the family of an ex-offender do not have any practical knowledge of these barriers and other challenges that sometimes make helping them a difficult process. This is why careful planning and preparation must precede any attempt to mentor the families of inmates in the prison system. Preparation for mentoring should include an understanding of the mentor role (see the chapter on *Mentoring*), knowledge of the systems that affect the family, and an understanding of the importance of addressing the abandonment issues that affect families. Too often, people think about mentoring in the sense of how good it would feel to help someone. They often falsely believe that people are going to automatically accept them with open arms. They also fail to recognize personal bias toward people of different economic status or race or fail to consider the impact that society and culture might play in the mentoring of families.

Usually when an individual is incarcerated, the family has come under the scrutiny of various social service agencies due to the loss of financial support. Consequently, they may view the mentor with skepticism, treating the mentor's intervention as just another intrusion in their lives.

If the mentors have limited experience with other ethnic groups, it is possible they may have unrealistic or inadequate expectations for that segment of the population. An example of this is when the mentor does not hold families to keeping appointments or following through with assignments, thereby allowing the family to see themselves more as victims than as worthwhile individuals who can and should take responsibility for their lives. Mentors should not be so ready to offer up excuses for inappropriate behavior simply because of an individual's ethnic or social background. Neither should a mentor expect families to live up to unrealistic or lofty expectations. Mentors must understand the family's need for validation of their self-worth and seek to encourage and support them in that endeavor, while reminding them that their struggling has the potential for growth.

Mentors must also remember that they have an obligation to keep their commitment to meet with the individual or family on a regular basis. Those who have suffered the loss of a loved one are often afraid to trust. So anyone who is interested in mentoring must understand that in order to build trust they are required to honor their commitment to these families.

In mentoring, it is important to remember that you are there to offer emotional and technical support. Often a mentor helps to provide the children with clothing and other items, although there can be a downside to this. One issue is that the children may see the mentors strictly for what they can give them financially, without being interested in the emotional or technical support. Another issue is that the help may contribute to a loss of self-esteem on the part of the adults in the family, due to their inability to provide for their family. Mentors have to remember that their role is not to serve as a surrogate parent but to provide emotional and technical support to the family.

Mentors must also understand the various systems and how they affect families. It is the loss of the support of these different systems that leads to the discouragement and ostracism of family members. For instance:

- The school system's support may be cut off because a teenager in the family drops out of school or misses a lot of school because he or she has to care for siblings or work to help support the family financially.

- The family is often isolated from other family members, which results in a closure of the family support system because of divided family loyalties due to a family member's incarceration.

- The family may become part of the social service system due to the need for financial or housing assistance.

- There may be closure of the community support system because the family has been forced to relocate to a place where they now have no ties to the community.

The availability or unavailability of these support systems leads to relationship problems within the family structure, and this is carried over into the working relationship with the mentor.

Mentoring an inmate's family, therefore, can be a complex and involved process. That being the case, we would recommend that anyone who wants to work with families not only recognize the above issues but also work side-by-side with a counselor who is trained to deal with families and recognizes the issues mentioned above and other issues that may arise. A detailed discussion of those issues is not the scope of this book; however, it is helpful for anyone who desires to help ex-offenders to recognize these family issues, as they could affect, either positively or negatively, progress in working with the inmate.

CHAPTER SIX

Addressing Other Vital Needs

In helping your loved one, you need to be aware of his ability to meet the following needs and be prepared with options in case he has no resources in these areas. Unless you have the skill and finances to meet the needs described below, it is best to search out a social service agency to help.

Food and clothing

Until your loved one is earning enough income to purchase his own food, he will need to depend upon the charity of others and you to provide him with daily sustenance. This does not necessarily mean that your loved one will have to depend upon soup kitchens, however. If your finances permit, certainly you should consider purchasing groceries for him until he is able to buy his own. If not, here are some suggestions:

- Check if there is a food bank in your community. America's Second Harvest, a domestic hunger-relief organization, has a network of over 200 food banks throughout the United States. (Their contact information is listed in the Appendix). Food banks collect surplus food donated from grocery stores, restaurants, etc., and distribute the food to people in need. Many food banks do not distribute directly to the public but to feeding programs that, in turn, distribute the food to the public. If your local food bank does not distribute to the public directly, they should be able to assist with names and contact information of their member agencies that distribute food directly to the public..

- Check with the churches in your area. Some of them offer hunger-relief efforts such as hot meals, distribution of groceries, and similar programs.

- Contact the agency in your state or city responsible for the administration of the federal Food Stamp Program. Information about this program is located in the Appendix.

- Check with friends and relatives. They may be willing to donate food.

The ex-offender should also have an adequate supply of clothing available when he or she leaves prison. In addition to the work-related clothing mentioned in the chapter on *Employment*, the ex-offender should have other walking-around clothing as well. See the *Employment* chapter for more information on clothing.

Medical treatment

You should be prepared to refer your loved one to the licensed medical treatment facilities that can address each of your loved one's medical needs. Some ex-offenders may be suffering from cancer, AIDS, physical impairments, or other injuries. Make it a point to determine, before your ex-offender gets out of prison, if he or she has any medical problems. Also see the section titled "Medical Needs" in the chapter on *Employment*.

Transportation

Unless your loved one is located in an urban area where there are buses, taxicabs, and/or subways available, he will need help with some sort of transportation to get to church, work, and other places until he can obtain his own transportation. Perhaps you would be willing to drive your loved one to and from work, to the grocery store, and to other essential places.

Be careful about getting your loved one a car to drive too soon after he is released from prison. The only exceptions would be if the ex-offender needs a car to perform his job—if he were a pizza-delivery person, for example, or if he lives in a remote place where it would not be easy to get around on public transportation.

Why do I mention a restriction on cars? Oftentimes an ex-offender's rehabilitation depends on him NOT having access to certain places and certain areas. If he has a car and is free to go where he pleases, what's to stop him from going back to the people and places that got him sent to prison in the first place? Also, cars carry with them a financial responsibility that may be too high for ex-offenders just starting to get their lives together.

Insurance, title, tags, and maintenance, even on an old car, can easily run over $250 a month, which requires an income just to maintain the vehicle.

Literacy and life skills training

Statistics from the US Department of Education show that 19% of incarcerated adults are functionally illiterate (compared with 4% of all adult Americans), and 40% of incarcerated adults are completely illiterate (compared with 21% of all adult Americans). The rate of people with learning disabilities in adult correctional facilities is also high at 11% (compared with 3% of all adult Americans). Therefore, the possibility of dealing with an ex-offender who cannot read or write well, if at all, is very likely. Any person involved with ex-offenders must recognize this fact and be prepared to deal with it. I have heard of churches that have brought illiterate ex-offenders into their congregations, given them Bibles, and enrolled them in Bible studies, not realizing the ex-offenders' inability to read the material. You should research educational programs in your community that work with adults with learning disabilities and provide literacy training. For spiritual education, Bibles on tape are excellent resources for individuals with below-average reading skills.

Substance abuse

In 1997, 21% of the sentenced state inmates were convicted of drug offenses. However, over 57% of sentenced state inmates were under the influence of alcohol or drugs at the time they committed their offense. Given these facts, it is highly likely that your loved one was involved with drugs before his incarceration.

Dealing with people on drugs is one of the things that you should not attempt to do without training or guidance from someone who is trained in substance abuse. If you need to locate someone who is trained as an addiction counselor, contact the National Association of Alcohol and Drug Abuse Counselors. (Their contact information is found in the Appendix).

I believe that drug and alcohol addictions are dangerous spirits that can be managed through various means but can only be broken through the power of God. Narcotics Anonymous (NA) and other similar 12-step groups, methadone treatment, and other management methods have been used with some degree of success. But, as many of the adherents to these programs will confirm, you will always be a drug addict, and you are never totally free.

However, I believe that Christ gives that freedom. A person who is freed from the bondage of drugs through faith and obedience in Jesus Christ can truly say that he is a "new creature, old things have passed away, and behold, all things become new" (2 Corinthians 5:17). Breaking the bondage of drugs means that there is no need for management methods anymore because the desire for the substance is gone.

Until the Spirit so moves, however, any person who is addicted to drugs is in bondage and needs to be managed to avoid destroying himself and others. Therefore, you need to be counseled as to the best way to handle a loved one who is currently addicted or has been addicted. Do not assume that because your loved one has not used drugs in a while that it means he is free. He is never truly free unless the bondage has been broken through Christ. Therefore, unless he shows the fruits and the manifestation of having had an encounter with the Lord in the area of his addiction, assume that he is at risk of getting hooked again.

It will be important to determine if this particular need exists (in conjunction with other medical needs as stated above) before trying to assist with the other needs. If the ex-offender is using substances (the fact that inmates are locked up does not mean that they do not have access to illegal substances), then it is important that he receive attention immediately. Develop a listing of organizations in your area that provide intervention for substance use and abuse. Many churches operate Christian programs based on 12-step principles. You may assist with other needs (such as food and clothing) temporarily, but I recommend not embarking on any long-term plan of action until the issue of substance use and abuse is addressed.

Other addictions
Your loved one may be suffering from other addictive behavior, such as an addiction to children, commonly manifested in pedophiles. Again, unless you have experience working with these populations, I would recommend that you seek professional help in dealing with them. And again, unless the Lord has broken the bondage of the addiction, you should assume that your loved one is still addicted and therefore likely, without intervention and management, to re-offend.

CHAPTER SEVEN

How Far Do I Go?

A man walks into a doctor's office with a broken right thumb. The doctor x-rays the thumb, determines where the break is, and then puts a cast on the thumb to make it immobile so that there is no further damage while it heals. The cast is a little inconvenient to the man since he has lost some of the function of his right hand. Nonetheless he must keep the cast on for four weeks, then return to the doctor for another x-ray.

After four weeks, the doctor removes the cast and then takes another x-ray. He determines that healing has not yet taken place, puts another cast on the thumb, and tells the man to return in another four weeks. Though it is terribly inconvenient, the man obliges. Four weeks later, he returns to the doctor's office. His thumb is x-rayed again. This time, the break has healed. The doctor tells the man to be careful with the thumb for a few more weeks, to give it time to strengthen. But the man no longer needs to return to the doctor. In another three weeks, the thumb has strengthened enough so that the man is able to resume normal physical activities.

Ex-offenders are much like that broken thumb. They need time to heal and time to strengthen. There is no set period that we can expect the ex-offender to have concluded the healing process; in fact, it may go on for years. But if he is healing properly, there should come a time when he no longer needs a doctor.

In other words, there should come a time where he no longer needs *you*.

I realize that is a strange statement. In fact, everyone needs *someone*. I need friends and family in my life. So do you. So we are never truly "self-sufficient." But your goal is for the ex-offender to heal enough to live his life without constantly needing to rely on you. He may need you to talk to when things get rough for him, or he may need you for emotional and spiritual support. But those times should become few and far between. In fact, when he is growing properly, he should become a source of strength and support for someone else.

There are times when a helper can delay or even block the ex-offender's healing progress. There are also times when the process of helping can backfire and prove detrimental to the helper. During these instances, it may be necessary to suspend or delay help until the situation is rectified.

In saying this, I am reminded of a scripture in the Bible in which Jesus lays down a process to follow in case a fellow believer ever wrongs you. Matthew 18:15-17 explains this process. But what I want to focus on is what Jesus says should be the last resort when a brother or sister continually offends (sins against) you. Jesus says, "let him be to you as a pagan or a tax collector."

If I were to depend on a literal reading of this scripture, Jesus is saying that after a brother or sister has been given several opportunities to repent of a sin against you and has not done so, that person should be as despised as a tax collector. That person is not to be trusted. No one would dare invite one over for dinner. People generally steer clear of people they despise. Jesus is clearly saying here that if a person continually sins against you and does not repent (turn from his sin), stay away from him!

Why would Jesus say this, especially since he ministers to tax collectors Matthew (Matthew 9:9) and Zacchaeus (Luke 19:1-10)? Because in each of these cases, the tax collectors repented, and in the case of Zacchaeus, reimbursed fourfold anyone he had cheated.

Sin is contagious. Sin has harmful effects not only on the sinner, but also on those against whom he is sinning. Jesus says we ought to stay away from sinners, both for our own protection, and for their protection. In doing this, the intention should not be to cast them away permanently, but for the sinner, through the separation, to realize the error of his ways and repent. The goal here is to restore the sinner, not to exile him. The choice as to whether restoration happens now lies in the hands of the sinner.

What about forgiveness? Doesn't the Bible say we are to forgive one another? Are we really forgiving if we treat brothers or sisters like they are walking leprosy?

There is a difference between forgiveness and allowing the practice of sin. What Jesus is speaking about in Matthew 18 is the practice of sin. Under no circumstances should we allow the practice of unrepented sin in our lives. Jesus is saying it is better to get away from such a person than to allow that sin to continue unabated.

Forgiveness, however, concerns the feelings in our hearts toward the person who is sinning. If there is unforgiveness in our hearts, we can harbor feelings of hatred, bitterness, and retaliation toward that person. This is just as bad as the sin and can cause the unforgiving person to respond according to bitterness and hate rather than redemption. Jesus is saying that our hearts should always be clear of unforgiveness, clear to receive the sinner back into our hearts and lives should he or she decide to repent. Jesus says that there should never be any limits on how many times we forgive, because in doing so, we free up our hearts from the damaging effects of hatred and bitterness.

So, you can forgive a sinner many times. In fact, you should always forgive, no matter whether he has repented or not. But you cannot allow a sinner to continue sinning against you, as it will have disastrous effects.

Many people think forgiving means *forgetting*, that forgiveness means to forget the sin ever happened. This is not what Scripture intends to convey. Forgiveness is an action of our own hearts that removes any enmity that exists between the sinner and us. But practically speaking, though we may forgive the sinner in our hearts, we cannot allow that sinner to continue practicing unabated.

There is another important point here to remember. The scripture in Matthew 18 does not say "if thy brother sins." It says "if thy brother sins *against thee*." I do not believe this scripture applies to every sin, simply because if it did, we would probably be treating everyone we know as tax collectors! But I believe this scripture can be translated as "if your brother or sister commits an act of sin that directly affects you."

Though all sins are offensive to God, there are varying degrees of how certain sins affect us. There are sins against society, such as selling drugs or polluting the environment, because these sins can affect large numbers of people and society at large. There are sins against church and family, which affect these groups at large. There are sins against other individuals, such as fornication or incest. And there are sins against self, such as smoking or eating a bad diet. In many cases, a sin can fall into two or more of these categories.

But Jesus is speaking here of those sins that affect you, either individually, as a member of society, or as a member of a family or church.

Having set the scriptural justification, I believe that there are certain things you should do in your relationship with an ex-offender that should not end, no matter what he does or says. However, because of the effects of sin, there are some reasons why you should cut off your support of an ex-offender in certain areas. I believe that under no circumstances should you continue to provide direct support to your loved one in the following instances unless you have prayed, sought counsel, and feel confident the Lord is leading you to do so:

1) When your loved one behaves in a way that puts you or those around you in harm or gets you caught up in illegal activities.

Your love for this person does not mean you have to coddle, make excuses for, or allow this person to continue to practice behavior that is illegal or emotionally, physically, or mentally harmful.

2) When your loved one becomes dependent on your support, rather than using it to make himself self-sufficient.

As I mentioned above, your goal is to provide support for healing to take place in your loved one's life. The more you provide support, the less he should be dependent on it.

I have seen people give to and support loved ones when it is clear that the loved one has no intention or desire to improve his life. This often happens because the person providing the support cannot bear to cut it off, out of fear that the loved one will not be able or is unwilling to take care of himself and will be hurt or destroyed. If you are in this predicament, I strongly urge you to seek counseling. You may be bearing a burden on your shoulders that you should not bear. In addition, cutting off your support may provide him with the motivation to help himself.

3) When your resources become depleted to the point where you are no longer able to care for your needs or those of your family.

Before getting into this situation it is best to count the costs and determine what you can do long- term and what you cannot. Then let your loved one know so that he does not feel letdown by the sudden cut off in support.

4) When your motives become selfish and impure.
In this instance, by all means, either change your motives or get away!

We once knew a woman who felt called to aftercare ministry. She signed up through her church to go into the prisons in Washington, DC, to minister to men and women who were scheduled to be released. After a few weeks of ministry, one ex-offender seemed to draw her attention more than the others did. Eventually she started mentoring him and making arrangements for his needs to be met upon release. She arranged for him to get an apartment and a job and picked him up every Sunday for church. Her efforts and his determination produced great success, as he was growing by leaps and bounds.

Two months later, while at work, he met a young lady and went out on a series of dates with her. When he shared this with his mentor, she seemed pleased and excited for him.

However, after that moment, her interest in him seemed to wane. She no longer picked him up for church. She tried to avoid him whenever they were at church. And she dropped out of the aftercare ministry altogether.

The ex-offender wondered for weeks why she stopped supporting him. After he talked with the pastor of his church, he discovered the reason.

The woman was not in the aftercare ministry to help ex-offenders. She was there to try to find a husband.

When the ex-offender found a romantic interest other than her, she felt dejected and hurt, even though their relationship was strictly non-romantic.

I stress the following strongly: Your mission in working with ex-offenders is to help them meet their God-given potential. If you are doing this because you hope to find a husband or wife, or a boyfriend or girlfriend, or hope to benefit financially, or want to put one more notch on your ministry belt, you may do more harm than good in the process.

The following are things you *should* do regardless of what the ex-offender has done or is doing. In some cases, doing the following may be all you *can* do. If that is the case, you need to understand that these things actually do lay a foundation for continued ministry. If this is *all* you can do, you are doing the *best* you can do.

Show unmerited and unlimited support for him by:

1) Praying for him on a regular basis.

2) Demonstrating that you still love him and care for him, no matter what happens or what he does.

3) Forgiving him for any wrong he has done, although you may choose to keep him away from you if he is

continuing to walk in sin that affects you or your family.

CHAPTER EIGHT

Your Loved One's Release Options

If your loved one has been released or is about to be released from prison, there are several release options that you need to be aware of. Knowing about these release options not only helps in pre-release planning but ensures that you can guide your loved one's assistance so that he does not violate any terms associated with his form of release.

What is parole?
Parole is a *privilege* given to offenders that allows them to spend their remaining sentence in the community. A granting of parole does not mean that the offender has served his or her entire sentence and is now free. An ex-offender on parole is still considered to be "on paper" and can be sent back to prison if he violates any of the provisions of his parole. An inmate is usually eligible for parole after he completes a minimum portion of his

sentence as prescribed by law. Special paroles are also granted for medical or geriatric reasons.

I mentioned before that parole is a privilege. It is not a legal right. There is no law that I am aware of that demands that a prisoner must be granted parole on a certain date or, indeed, at all. In most states, a committee or board or a governor or judge is given the authority to make parole decisions. This paroling body or person usually has to follow some guidelines, but most guidelines allow the paroling body to circumvent the guidelines if needed and make a decision based on discretion. In other words, when it comes to parole decisions, the offender is at the mercy of the paroling authority. Never mind that he has served ten years without a single disciplinary action, and that he has done his time clean. If the paroling authority *feels* that he is a risk to the community, his parole will not be granted. And with the public's increasing desire to punish criminals, and the sweeping changes in the law that result in prisoners doing more time for the same crimes, parole is even less likely to be granted.

How does my loved one prepare for a parole hearing?
The best way to prepare for a parole hearing is to for him to do his time clean. Society, the prison guards, the warden, and the parole board are all inclined *not* to believe anything offenders say. So the best policy is for him to put himself in a position where he does not have to answer for anything. He should do his time clean, avoid conflict and fights, and be respectful to everyone.

The next best thing is for him to take responsibility for his actions. If he did the crime, take responsibility for it. If he did the crime, and the paroling authorities think he did the crime, and he walks into the parole hearing and adamantly denies that he did the crime, guess who will be walking out of the room with a parole denial? If he did it, he should confess to it. He's already serving the time, so what purpose will it serve to deny it further? (If his conviction or sentence is under legal action, or if he is involved with any other unresolved legal action, he might want to consult with an attorney before implementing this step).

The only liability here is that if he has engaged in a long pattern of denial, the paroling authorities might find his confession to be less than genuine and think that he is only telling them what they want to hear.

Many paroling authorities use a scoring system that helps them determine the likelihood that the offender will re-offend. Contact the paroling authorities that are responsible for your loved one's parole decision and find out how they make decisions. If a scoring system is used, find out what it is. This information is usually public knowledge.

Preparing for a parole hearing also involves putting together a parole plan. A parole plan, simply put, tells the paroling authorities what steps he will implement to get his life together if they decide to let him leave prison. The parole plan must include the following:

1) Plans for housing arrangements.

2) Plans for food and clothing and transportation upon release.

3) Plans for drug or alcohol rehabilitation or treatment, if his crime involved the abuse of any substance.

4) Plans for obtaining a job, or getting vocational training, or other education leading to employment.

5) Plans for income maintenance, if he is disabled and unable to work.

6) Plans for taking care of his spouse and/or minor children.

7) Plans for dealing with any outstanding charges he may have.

8) Plans for dealing with any personality disorders or sicknesses, i.e., anger management, mental illness, depression, etc.

9) Plans for caring for any medical needs.

10) Friends, family, or agencies in the community that are willing to help with post-release needs and issues. If you are a family member or a friend willing to provide support in some area, write a letter to the paroling authorities indicating your support. In some jurisdictions, paroling authorities will even allow meetings before the parole hearing.

11) Plans to pay off any fines or other pending financial obligations.

The paroling authorities want to make sure that your loved one has a blueprint for success once he is released. All the components of this plan should be put in place before the parole hearing (the case manager or counselor in the prison can assist with this), and a copy of the plan should be placed in his parole jacket so that it can be reviewed prior to the hearing. Understand, however, that he will be judged not only on the effectiveness of the plan, but also on whether he has the wherewithal to implement it. He may have the best plan in the world, but if the paroling authorities feel he cannot or will not follow through with it once he is released, he will not be granted parole.

Even after following all these instructions and doing the right things, he still may not be granted parole. Sometimes, parole decisions are based upon external factors, such as prison overcrowding, public reaction to his crime, the feelings and recommendations of the victims and/or their families, political pressure, etc. With all of these factors, parole can seem drastically unfair. The only thing you can do is make sure that your loved one puts himself in the right position to be granted a favorable decision.

Probation

Probation is slightly different from parole. While parole decisions are often made by a paroling authority and usually follow the time served of some portion of a prison sentence, a judge can levy probation as an alternative to sentencing. A person on probation will have to adhere to conditions similar to those of a person on parole. If he violates those conditions, he may be held liable for the sentence as imposed by law. Nationwide, there are 4,074,000 men and women on probation, as opposed to 774,600 on parole.

Supervised release
Supervised release is similar to parole in that it takes place after the completion of a prison sentence. However, supervised release is usually levied by a judge at sentencing time and follows a specific period of imprisonment. For example, an inmate who is sentenced to ten years of imprisonment, followed by three years of supervised release, will have to serve the entire ten years (minus any sentence reduction), and then serve the three years in the community. Supervised release has replaced parole in many areas of the United States. Probation or parole officers typically perform the supervision.

Direct or final discharge
Direct or final discharge occurs when the inmate has served the entire sentence prescribed by law (including any sentence served on parole and on supervised release). At this point, he is legally entitled to be released from prison. He is then considered to be a free man and no longer has to answer to parole or probation authorities, as is the case with other forms of release.

With direct discharge, an ex-offender cannot be sent back to prison unless he commits another crime and is tried and sentenced according to the law. Under the other forms of release, an ex-offender can be sent back to prison for not finding a job, for congregating in drug-infested areas, for consuming alcohol, or even for not being at home at a prescribed curfew time.

Direct discharge does not mean that an ex-offender can relax and do whatever he wants. Having been branded with a prison sentence, the ex-offender is much more likely to be re-arrested, tried and convicted, even if he didn't do anything, because law enforcement personnel know that ex-offenders are more likely to re-offend.

Mandatory release

The law in many states grants mandatory release after an offender has served his sentence minus any credits earned for "good" time. For instance, an offender may get a year knocked off his sentence for doing his time clean, with no significant violation of prison rules. An offender on mandatory release is placed under some type of supervision until the expiration of his sentence.

Rescinding of sentence

Once a sentence is imposed on a person by a judge or magistrate, only a judge or magistrate can reverse that decision. Parole authorities, prison officials, and probation officers have no power to increase or decrease a sentence. Therefore, if there is some legal dispute about your loved one's sentence, a judge may decide to rescind the sentence and allow your loved one to go free. A judge may decide, however, to allow probation or some other sanction instead of the sentence.

Pardons and commutations

In state correctional systems, the governor of the state usually grants pardons and commutations. . For federal charges, the president of the United States has the power to grant pardons and commutations. A pardon is simply the government's way of saying that the offender is forgiven for the crime he has committed and is no longer bound to serve the sentence imposed. (We

Christians should understand that concept well!) A commutation does not involve forgiveness for the crime but the reduction of the penalty for the crime to a lesser one. For instance, an offender serving a life term in prison might have his sentence commuted to 25 years, allowing him to be released from prison in the future.

CHAPTER NINE

Mentoring

Mentor is a Greek term meaning "adviser" or "wise person." Mentoring brings a personal approach to aftercare by providing trusted and wise Christian advisers to ex-offenders to help them deal with life on the outside. A mentor can be a very helpful source of information, encouragement, spiritual support, or just someone to talk to.

Mentors are responsible for providing support, encouragement, and guidance to ex-offenders by meeting with them regularly to listen and share knowledge and experience.

I would strongly recommend that every ex-offender be evaluated and considered for a match with a mentor before he is released from prison or as soon as possible after release. Whether you, or someone else, are considering serving as a mentor, it is important to understand fully what the mentoring relationship entails. Below, I will go into some detail describing this wonderful relationship that will bless not only the protégé but also the mentor.

Qualifications for ex-offenders

Although mentoring is a very important aspect of re-entry into the community, not every ex-offender is an ideal candidate for a mentoring match. For instance, if an ex-offender has a mental illness, he is best dealt with in an institutional or professional environment. Also, ex-offenders who do not desire to be mentored are obviously not a good choice—you cannot force anyone to do anything. In our mentoring program at CORM, we review and assess each candidate to determine whether he would be a good match for a mentor. Following are the criteria we ask inmates to meet before they are assigned a mentor:

Inmates eligible for matches

- Must go through training and a correspondence course to ensure that they understand what a mentor is and the benefits of the mentor relationship.

- Must be guaranteed parole or probation release.

- Must be reasonably compliant with the program and with prison rules up until a mentor is assigned.

- Must understand and be willing to submit to the fact that this is a Christian mentoring program.

Qualifications for mentors

We also ask that mentors meet certain qualifications. They are as follows:

- Must believe in the program and the participant.

The last thing we want is a mentor who has beliefs that are contrary to what our program is all about. We want people who believe that all men, regardless of what they have done, are candidates for the grace and mercy of God. We want people who are not punitive-minded but restorative-minded. We want people who, if they had to choose between locking an inmate up and rehabilitating him, would choose to rehabilitate.

- Must be relationship-oriented.

Mentoring is, first of all, a relationship. It is not a program with an agenda and a set number of hours. Mentors realize that the person they are being assigned is a friend who may call them at midnight if he has a problem.

- Must understand ex-offenders and the problems they face.

Ex-offenders have problems that most of us who have never been to prison will never face. It is helpful in a mentoring relationship that the mentor has some understanding or knowledge of the struggles that are faced by ex-offenders, so he can address those issues when meeting with his protégé.

- Must be able to encourage and support without creating dependency.

As a mentor, you may be the most important person in the ex-offender's life. But should you, for whatever reason, no longer able be to mentor, the ex-offender should not be so dependent upon you that he cannot move on with his life and establish a relationship with another mentor, if needed.

- Must be a responsible Christian fellowshipping regularly with a local church.

Now, is this necessary? Do you have to be a Christian to mentor someone? No, you don't. But it may be helpful to read the chapter titled *Preparing Yourself* for the wisdom behind this.

- Must be drug-free and crime-free for at least one year prior to appointment.

You cannot help someone keep himself free from substance abuse and crime if you have not proven yourself able to do it. One year of crime-free and drug-free behavior is the absolute minimum.

- Must reside in or near the town or locality where the ex-offender resides.

Being a mentor involves not just chatting on the phone and sending letters but also meeting personally one-on-one weekly with the ex-offender. You may not be able to do that if you live in California and the ex-offender lives in Texas, unless you want a lot of frequent flyer miles.

Steps toward matching a mentor with an ex-offender

- First step

The mentor must be trained. Some people believe they are naturally good with people and at building relationships and do not need training. Do not make that assumption. The purpose of training is not to tell you how to build a relationship, but to educate you on the issues involved in dealing with ex-offenders and to inform you of the commitment that will be required. Check with the national ministries listed in the Appendix of this book. Some of them offer mentor-training courses.

- Second step

Make a decision. The mentor must decide that this is something he wants to do. The decision should take into consideration his family, his church, and his other responsibilities.

- Third step

Have him complete an application, undergo a background investigation, and provide two references, including one from his pastor. Unless you know someone who can serve as a mentor to your loved one, and know him well, I would recommend checking the following to ensure that you know who you are dealing with:

(1) Criminal history—Has he been arrested, imprisoned, put on probation? If so, what for? This information is important not only to guarantee that you do not have someone newly released from prison mentoring your loved one, but to also ensure that your loved one meets any restrictions on fraternizing with offenders or ex-offenders.

(2) Involvement with church home—Which church does he attend? Does he attend often? Is he involved with church activities? Does the pastor know him? Would the pastor recommend him for mentoring?

(3) Employment—Is he able to work? If so, does he have a job, does he operate a legitimate business, is he retired, or does he attend school? Has he been employed for a while? Is he a good employee? If the person whom you are considering to mentor your loved

one does not have a job and has no good reason for not having one, tell him thank you for his time and move on. A person without a job will not be a good example and role model for an ex-offender.

- Fourth Step

Introduce ex-offender to his mentor personally. Monitor the relationship to ensure all is going well.

Aspects of the mentoring process

<u>Criteria for mentor matches</u>
In our ministry, matches are made taking into consideration the case history of the protégé and the information provided by the mentor. This ensures that the most compatible matches are made. However, under no circumstances are the following matches made. We recommend that you adhere to the same criteria.

1) Men matched with women, and vice versa.

2) Older protégés matched with significantly younger mentors.

3) Interstate mentoring relationships; i.e., mentor living in a different state or city from the protégé where the distance prevents the mentor spending one-on-one time with the protégé.

4) Any match that would violate the conditions of the protégé's parole or probation release.

5) Any match that could hinder the protégé's growth and development in the word of God.

Responsibilities and habits of a good mentor

1. *Remain in contact with the ex-offender.*

Initiates and maintains contact with the ex-offender while in prison and after release. Encourages the ex-offender to feel free to call him after release. Does not develop a habit of expecting the ex-offender to initiate contact with him. Makes the effort of remaining in contact with the protégé.

2. *Visit participant in prison.*

If the ex-offender is still in prison, visits the ex-offender as often as he is able. Visits at least once a month before release, in order to develop relationship before the offender hits the streets. If the offender is incarcerated in an out-of-state prison, writes letters to the offender in lieu of visitation.

3. *Call and/or visit participant once a week when he or she has been released.*

Weekly contact is very essential. Oftentimes, ex-offenders can become easily distracted and lose their focus. Weekly contact enables the mentor to keep the ex-offender on the right track and to keep him or her focused.

4. *Maintain contact with participant for a minimum of six months.*

Upon agreement by both parties, regular contact can be continued past the six-month period. We usually recommend a year or more, with a goal that the relationships that are built as a result of mentoring continue for many years beyond.

5. *Help the participant develop a life plan and obtain resources necessary for survival; give general support as*

the participant goes through with his or her plan.
Each ex-offender who participates in mentoring must have goals for his or her life. A life lived aimlessly and without purpose will surely lead the ex-offender into trouble. The mentor must help the ex-offender establish short-term and long-term goals and hold the ex-offender accountable for meeting them. I emphasize here that the mentor must *help*, not *dictate*. Ultimately, the ex-offender must decide what to do with his or her own life.

6. *Try to avoid personal financial involvement.*
Do not give the ex-offender any money, if possible. This is an important rule. Sometimes ex-offenders will accept mentors with the intent of taking advantage or manipulating, or will continue relationships only because they are financially expedient. This rule lets them know that mentors are not free meal tickets but friends who are willing to help during a difficult adjustment period.

However, there is a flip side of the coin. I knew a gentleman who was mentoring an ex-offender who had just been released from a prison in Virginia. He knew the ex-offender was only trying to get handouts from him. So, every time the ex-offender called him to get some money, he agreed to give it to him — provided the ex-offender sat down with him for an hour and studied the Bible with him. After about six or seven sessions this way, the ex-offender would continue to call but would not ask for any money. He just called because he enjoyed the Bible study and wanted to study more! Soon, the ex-offender accepted the Lord and started going to church with his mentor.

Sometimes money can be used in this way. I heard one

preacher say that it is possible to "buy" a sinner out of the world and into the Kingdom. But generally, unless you have deep pockets and can afford to slip your protégé a few bucks constantly until he demonstrates the fruit of your labors, I wouldn't set a precedent.

7. *Pray regularly for the ex-offender and study the Bible with him or her.*

If the ex-offender is a Christian, a good mentor studies the Bible with him or her regularly and prays with and for the offender on a regular basis.

8. *Look for opportunities to minister the gospel.*

If the ex-offender is not a Christian, then a good mentor demonstrates the love of Christ at all times and looks for an opportunity to share Christ with him.

CHAPTER TEN

Getting a Good Christian Support Base

A dry log, if left in the flame long enough, will eventually catch fire.

Ex-offenders are like those dry logs. If you keep them in the flame of God's presence on a regular basis, eventually they will conflagrate into mighty fires for God's glory.

But Satan always likes to throw a little water on the log from time to time, to keep it damp enough so that it never catches fire. And if the log is ever removed from the fire...

As simplistic as it sounds, that is exactly what your loved one will encounter in spiritual realms. This chapter will look at ways that you can help keep your loved one in the presence of God on a regular basis.

Getting the ex-offender to attend church on a regular basis is important. But it involves more than just going to worship services. In fact, little growth in an ex-offender's life happens in worship services. The average Christian spends about two hours a week in congregational gatherings. The focus of this chapter is on how to keep him girded during the other 166 hours of the week.

The following are some things that I suggest to help your ex-offender build a strong foundation in Christ. I stress that you should not try to force any of these things on him but instead gently encourage him to do them.

1) Get him in a good, Biblically based Bible study at least once a week.

The benefit of Bible study is that it allows the type of learning interchange that seldom happens in worship services. In a Bible study, a student can follow a curriculum, ask questions, and get to know his fellow Bible study students.

2) Study the Bible personally with him.

Class-based Bible study is one thing. Personal Bible study is another. Studying the Bible with him will allow the ex-offender to raise those issues, questions, or concerns that he may not feel comfortable sharing in a classroom setting.

3) Fill his musical repertoire with Christian songs.

Okay, so he's been grooving on P. Diddy or Limp Bizkit for the past few years, and it seems as if he just won't stop. Suggest to him a few Christian songs that he can listen to. Buy him tapes, tune in to Christian radio stations, and encourage him to listen to them. Take him to Christian concerts. I believe that there are evil spirits inherent in many of the worldly songs today, which is all the more reason why you should gently guide him away from that stuff.

4) Get him in a good Christian support group, particularly one that deals with life-controlling behaviors or other issues that ex-offenders deal with.

This is an added dimension to going to the Bible study or going to worship services. Most of us who have never been to prison have not the faintest idea of what it is like, both in prison and afterwards. As well-meaning as we are, we cannot identify with him. A support group of persons struggling with the same things can strengthen him and help him to realize that he is not alone in his struggle.

5) Rid his environment of all evil influences wherever possible.

The less evil there is to distract your loved one, the less likely he will be tempted to partake. If possible (and with his permission), rid his environment of pornography (on TV and in print), violent movies, tapes, books, images, or artifacts, anything representing an idol, drugs, alcohol, etc. Even certain friends, if they are an evil influence, may need to steer clear.

6) Pray with him regularly and encourage him to pray often.

7) Involve him in any spiritual activity you may be a part of.

If you go to see an inspiring Christian drama, take him with you. If you go to hear a renowned Christian speaker, invite him along. Again, the less he is out of the fire, the less opportunity Satan will have to get him sopping wet.

8) Try, as best as you can, to expose him to a Christian environment.

If your local churches have job openings, have him apply for these jobs before he applies for any others. Encourage him to eat at restaurants patronized by Christians. While looking for resources for him, search out Christian transitional homes, Christian shelters, and Christian halfway houses.

9) Get him a mentor.
See the chapter on *Mentoring*.

CHAPTER ELEVEN

Housing

Probably one of your greatest concerns about your loved one is where he will stay upon his release from prison. This is almost as big an issue as employment,. Because your loved one is an ex-offender, he will find a diminished pool of available housing. In some jurisdictions, ex-offenders are released from prison with no money and no resources, so it is unlikely that he'll get an apartment within a few hours after getting out.

Statistics gathered by CORM indicates that a majority of ex-offenders stay with friends or family after being released. If there are no friends or family willing or able to offer housing, ex-offenders often stay on the streets or at emergency shelters. There is a small percentage of ex-offenders in in-patient treatment centers or transitional housing.

If you are willing and able to offer your loved one long-term housing, then I will save you the time and effort it takes to read this chapter—move on to the next one. But if your loved one needs a place to stay upon release from prison, or if you are able to offer housing for only a limited time, read on.

In locating housing for an ex-offender, there are four primary concerns: *cost, environment, expected occupancy date*, and whether there will be a *background check* conducted.

Cost
If your loved one has no income, and you are not able to provide housing for him, then obviously he needs to find either free or low-cost housing, at least until he can find employment.

Environment
An ex-offender has to be careful about the environment he is placed in. One reason is because his parole certificate may say so. Many parole or probation authorities require the ex-offender to stay away from known offenders and from areas where criminal activity, such as selling or using drugs, is taking place. Another reason is that even if a criminal environment is not an issue, the ex-offender can be placed in an environment that is non-supportive, hostile, or detrimental to the ex-offender's growth. I have seen ex-offenders thrust into some pressure-cooker situations. I know one who left a halfway house and, with no job, moved into the home of his girlfriend, with whom he had three children. The girlfriend was not faithful, and she would be away from the house for long periods of time while he looked after the children. She stopped paying the bills and put pressure on him to get a job and pay the bills around the house. She would frequently scold him whenever he

did something wrong. All of this transpired within three weeks after he left prison. He was, like many ex-offenders, thrust into the role of caretaker, without having the time to take care of himself. He responded to the pressure by taking drugs. Eventually he failed a urinalysis and went back to prison.

Sometimes these situations cannot be prevented. But we do an injustice to ex-offenders if we put them in pressure-cooker situations without any preparation.

Expected occupancy date

In searching for housing, it is important to know how long it will be before your loved one can move in. This will help for planning purposes. Only a few of the options below offer immediate occupancy, meaning you will be allowed to move in within twenty-four hours of the request.

Background checks

Many housing options will conduct a background check or ask questions about any criminal past. Just as there are those who will discriminate against an ex-offender in hiring because of his criminal past, there are those who will do the same in granting a lease or even extending a mortgage. More about this later.

Housing options

Transitional housing

- Cost: *Free or minimal cost*
- Environment: *Usually favorable*
- Expected Occupancy Date: *Depends on facility and availability of rooms, but usually do not allow people to stay on an emergency basis*

- Background Checks: *Usually none conducted*
- Length of stay: *Usually a few months, typically no more than a year*

For ex-offenders who cannot stay with friends or relatives and cannot afford their own lodging, this is the next-best bet. For the purposes of this section, I define transitional housing as any housing arrangement that allows residents to stay for a fixed period of time, usually six months to a year, while offering services geared to helping the ex-offender enter successfully into society. Good transitional homes have a controlled environment and do not allow substance abuse or other detrimental behaviors within the facility. Some transitional housing options have free or reduced rent based upon a percentage of the resident's income. Many only admit residents with particular problems (such as drug abuse, alcoholism, homelessness, etc.). Many require the resident to get a job either before or soon after admission.

The most popular type of transitional homes geared to ex-offenders are called halfway houses. These homes usually admit ex-offenders directly from jail or prison, and are usually operated by or contracted by the state. Contact your state's Department of Corrections to find out what halfway houses exist in your state and what is required for admission.

Many private organizations and churches are establishing homes for ex-offenders as well. Finding these homes will take some research. Check with the chaplains in your state correctional facility. Also, check with the national organizations that are listed in the Appendix of this book. In addition, check with your state or city zoning or regulatory office, since many of these homes, because of their clientele, have to be registered or licensed under a special designation, such as "halfway home", "community residence facility", or "adult rehabilitation home." (See Rehabilitation homes, below).

Rooming houses
- Cost: *Varies*
- Environment: *Depends on the rooming house*
- Expected Occupancy Date: *Varies depending on the rooming house proprietor and the availability of rooms*
- Background checks: *Usually none conducted, although this depends upon the rooming house operator*
- Length of stay: *Indefinite*

This is another option for an ex-offender who has income. Rooming houses typically offer a room and shared facilities for a set price per week. This definition also includes private homes in which rooms or other portions of the home are offered for rent or other compensation. Many will not inquire as to the roomer's background, making this ideal for an ex-offender. This is cheaper than a hotel or motel, but it has its drawbacks.

Rooming houses offer no services, only a room. In many rooming houses, there is no guarantee as to the environment the ex-offender will be subject to. Some rooming houses are shady places, and if your loved one is susceptible to succumbing to negative behavior, this may not be a good option. Not to say that there are no good rooming houses, but the good ones come with a price. You get what you pay for.

Hotels and motels
- Cost: *Usually expensive*
- Environment: *Usually favorable, although some hotels can have a seedy environment*
- Expected Occupancy Date: *Immediate, unless the facility has no rooms available*
- Background Checks: *Usually not conducted*
- Length of stay: *Usually short-term*

Depending on the facility, hotels and motels may offer a better environment than a rooming house, but that is not guaranteed. No services are offered other than those typically offered to hotel guests, such as room service.

Hotels and motels are intended only for short-term stays. Spending a month or longer in a hotel may cost you as much as or more than if you had rented an apartment. But this is a good option for an ex-offender who has income and wants a place to stay, pending finding an apartment or other permanent arrangements.

Emergency shelters
- Cost: *Usually free or minimal cost*
- Environment: *Varies*
- Expected Occupancy Date: *Immediate, during the shelters' intake hours*
- Background Checks: *Never performed*
- Length of stay: *Usually overnight*

This is usually the housing option an ex-offender has to rely on when all else has failed. Emergency shelters usually offer a bed, and shower, and maybe food, usually overnight. In typical shelters, the resident must leave in the morning.

Some emergency shelters have support programs and can be a great resource for offenders who have no place else to go. Many people, however, detest shelters, mainly because of the stigma of homelessness attached to them and because some of them are crime-ridden. But for an ex-offender who needs shelter in a hurry, such as within a few days or a few hours, the emergency shelter may be the best option, since the other options on this list may require some lead-time before the ex-offender can take residence.

Check with your local government for a list of shelters in your area. There may be a central agency or office that conducts intake.

Rehabilitation homes
- Cost: *Usually free, but some charge a fee*
- Environment: *Favorable*
- Expected Occupancy Date: *Varies depending upon room or bed availability*
- Background Checks: *Sometimes performed*
- Length of stay: *Few days to several years*

A rehabilitation home offers treatment and support services for ailments such as substance abuse, medical conditions, disabilities, or mental illnesses. The length of stay may vary from a few days to several years, depending upon the resident's condition. Your local health department will have information on these houses, since they usually have to be licensed as health care facilities. While these houses offer shelter, their primary purpose is treating an underlying condition that may result in or contribute to homelessness. They should not be sought out strictly for shelter. But if your loved one has a medical, mental, or familial condition that requires treatment, these homes may be the best option.

Friends and family
- Cost: *Varies*
- Environment: *Varies*
- Expected Occupancy Date: *Varies*
- Background checks: *Almost never conducted*
- Length of stay: *As long as they will allow*

It would seem that staying with a friend or family member would be one of the best options for an ex-offender. After all, isn't the camaraderie of a friend or the care and concern of a family member the best environment to be in? This is true in many instances. However, in just as many instances, this can be a disaster.

Staying with a friend or family member does not keep the ex-offender from getting himself into an unfavorable environment. Issues concerning criminal activity and pressure-cooker situations can occur as easily in a friend or family living situation as in any other. Make sure your loved one is in an environment that is positive and productive rather than destructive.

Although a friend or family member may roll out the red carpet and tell your loved one that he can stay as long as he wants, don't count on it. It is always best in these situations to treat this living situation as a temporary one and make plans to move to more permanent housing. He should never wait until he wears out his welcome.

I am reminded of a male ex-offender who got out of prison and moved in with his best buddy from high school. His buddy had his own one-bedroom apartment, and the ex-offender slept on the couch. Two months later, the ex-offender's best buddy met a gorgeous young lady at a party and started to date her. The young lady, it seems, had a rocky relationship with her parents and needed to move out of their house, where she was living.

A week later, guess who got the boot?

Churches and religious facilities
- Cost: *Varies*
- Environment: *Can be favorable depending on the pastor and the congregation*
- Expected Occupancy Date: *If a room is available, usually immediately, unless the church or religious facility has some criteria that the resident must meet before moving in*
- Background checks: *Usually not performed formally*
- Length of stay: *Varies*

Churches in your area may have rooms or larger churches may have apartments that they offer to persons who need short-term or long-term shelter. The shelter is usually offered for a fee or in exchange for some small jobs done around the church, such as cleaning or clerical work. The church may restrict certain behaviors, such as smoking, drinking alcohol, and having women over to the room while residing at the church. Contact the pastors in your area for information about the availability of church-run shelter.

While it would seem like the church would be an ideal environment for the ex-offender, in some cases it is not. A pastor or a congregation that looks down on or is suspicious of ex-offenders may cause their resident more grief than joy and cause him to want to seek shelter elsewhere.

Apartments

- Cost: *Varies*
- Environment: *Varies*
- Expected Occupancy Date: *Varies, but immediate occupancy is usually not offered*
- Background checks: *Sometimes conducted; depends on the landlord*
- Length of stay: *As long as the rent is paid*

Apartments offer more independence and privacy that any of the previous housing options. However, the typical ex-offender may need to rely upon one or more of the previous housing options before getting to this point. Seldom is an ex-offender ready to assume his own apartment straight out of prison, unless he has money stashed away.

Though apartments offer true independent living and more privacy, the environment in many apartment houses can still be detrimental. Also, some landlords will conduct a background check or ask about any criminal history.

Private homes

- Cost: *Varies*
- Environment: *Not an issue*

- Expected Occupancy Date: *Renting usually brings quicker occupancy than purchasing, although neither option can be counted on for immediate occupancy*
- Background checks: *May be conducted by homeowner or mortgage lender*
- Length of stay: *As long as the rent or mortgage is paid*

This option offers more independence and privacy than the apartment house, and the environment is not an issue since the ex-offender controls the environment. Private homes can be bought or rented, and are usually an option only after one or more of the above options have been pursued.

Private homes also carry a higher degree of responsibility than the other housing options. Typically, the ex-offender will have to pay for utilities, keep the lawn well-manicured, keep the sidewalk free of snow, etc. Make sure that your loved one can handle that level of responsibility before considering this option.

Housing discrimination[1]

The Fair Housing Act prohibits discrimination in granting or terminating tenancies in renting housing or in selling homes. Generally, a landlord cannot discriminate in selecting residents based upon race, religion, disability, or age. However, a landlord can legally deny housing to an ex-offender because of his criminal past.

---

[1] Information in this section is adapted from *Every Landlord's Legal Guide*, 4th ed., by Marcia Stewart, Janet Portman and Ralph Warner (Nolo.com, July 2000).

There are a few exceptions to this law that you should be aware of.

Prior drug use
If an ex-offender has a history of drug use (whether or not he was convicted) but no current involvement, he is considered disabled under the Fair Housing Amendments Act. A refusal to provide housing based upon his prior drug use is illegal. However, if he was involved in the sale or distribution of drugs, he is not protected under federal law.

Arrests but no convictions
Since our legal system presumes an arrestee to be innocent until proven guilty, it is illegal for a housing provider to refuse to provide housing based upon an arrest record without convictions.

Exemptions
Exemptions to the Fair Housing Act and the Fair Housing Amendments Act include the following:

- Owner-occupied buildings with four units or less.

- Single-family housing rented without the use of discriminatory advertising or a real estate broker.

- Certain residences operated by religious organizations and private clubs that limit occupancy to their own members.

- In the case of age discrimination, housing reserved solely for senior citizens.

In some cases, states have their own implementations of these laws. Check with your state's housing department.

CHAPTER TWELVE

Assistance with Employment

One of the biggest struggles that a typical ex-offender will have upon release from prison is finding and/or keeping a job. The following factors can contribute to the difficulty. Advice on how to help your loved one overcome them follows.

1) Lack of job skills or education
2) Lack of ability to present oneself effectively
3) Reluctance of employers to hire ex-offenders
4) Lack of desire to work
5) Medical problems
6) Unavailability of adequate employment

Lack of job skills or education
Statistics show that the typical ex-offender has little education. Many ex-offenders have never graduated from high school. Those that have graduated have never attended or graduated from college. The typical

ex-offender starts to manifest serious criminal or delinquent activity in his teenage years, usually before graduating from high school. Needless to say, the typical ex-offender has very little job experience that he can place on a resume.

Ex-offenders in this situation are often relegated to low-paying, low-skilled jobs — hard work for very little pay.

If your loved one has not yet been released from prison, then he should be encouraged to take advantage of every educational opportunity that is offered in the prison or jail. Many will gladly do this, since it offsets boredom in the prisons and gives them something to do. The more educational certifications and diplomas that he is armed with when he gets out of prison, the better.

If there are no educational opportunities available in the prison where your loved one is incarcerated, don't be surprised. Modern prisons have pretty much deteriorated from rehabilitation to containment. In other words, their primary mission is to keep your loved one out of society until he has paid for his crime. Their secondary mission is to make money while doing it. The reverse is true with private prisons that are run by for-profit businesses, although government-run prisons are certainly guilty of this as well. And whenever costs need to be cut, or the bottom line is not looking as good as it did last year, the first things to go are the programs that are designed to help the ex-offender upon release. I have even heard one department of corrections director say openly that his job was not to make ex-offenders better. His job was to keep them off the streets until they have been punished to everyone's satisfaction.

If the prison where your loved one is incarcerated has no educational opportunities (or the ones there are sorely lacking in quality), don't be surprised. But don't be tolerant, either. Write letters to the warden and the director of the department of corrections. Write letters to your governor demanding that the prison where your loved one is incarcerated bring in educational programs for the inmates. If your state has a CURE (Citizens United for Rehabilitation of Errants) chapter, I strongly advise you join it and become involved. There's a good chance that if the prison in your state has inadequate or nonexistent educational opportunities, there's someone in your local CURE chapter who is working on the issue.

If the ex-offender or you are blessed enough to be able to afford it, the next best direction would be to get the ex-offender into some vocational training after he is released. If you cannot afford to pay for vocational training, check with your local, state, or federal labor department to see if they have free or low-cost training courses. Obviously the ex-offender will need clothes, food, shelter, and transportation, so those needs should be met before pursuing this option. Also, if the offender does not have a high school diploma or GED, now is the time for him to get one. Check with your state education office about your state's GED options. Illiteracy is also a problem for some offenders, so you will want to address this issue by checking with your state education office about courses to address this problem. It is best that all of these problems are addressed before the ex-offender seeks employment, if his shelter, food, clothing, and other arrangements will be stable during the amount of time it takes to address these problems.

Also, before pursuing this option, check with the ex-offender's parole or probation officer. Sometimes parole or probation authorities require the ex-offender to get a job within a set period of time following release. This is especially the case if the offender is in a halfway home.

If, for whatever reason, training is not an option, then follow my strategy, which is to get them into whatever job they can perform, no matter how low the pay, no matter how hard the work. Ex-offenders often are forced to rebuild their lives from the bottom up. Occasionally an ex-offender will land a job in a front office making fifteen dollars an hour. Sometimes you will hear of an ex-offender who came out of prison and went straight into his own business, earning a lot of money. While these stories are wonderful and encouraging, the average offender winds up swilling toilets or moving boxes for a living.

Once the ex-offender lands a job, he can then work on getting a better job, using the work record, experience, and skills he gained on the first one. The value of employment goes beyond just the paycheck. Employers look for an ability to keep regular hours at work and an ability to show himself trustworthy. Getting an ex-offender into any job as soon as possible means it will be that much sooner that he can build his skills set and start putting some effective work experience on his resume. I recommend that an ex-offender works at least a year on one job before branching out to other employment.

To do this effectively, it is recommended that you sit down with your loved one and develop some goals and objectives. If the ex-offender is getting a job just because he knows he needs to get one, or because the parole officer is bugging him, or because he needs the money, then the motivation is not strong enough. Every move he makes needs to be a step up the ladder toward a goal or objective that he has set for his life. What does he want to do? Get a house of his own? Get married? Have children? Have a nice car? Have a job that he loves and looks forward to getting up in the morning and going to? It is helpful that he realizes that he is not just working for the good of society or to appease his parole officer, but that he is working to achieve some real, substantive goals in his life.

Lack of ability to present oneself effectively

Today's job market is all about competition. Every time a job seeker sits across the desk from a potential employer and interviews for a position, he is literally trying to extend the job search of several others who are interviewing for the same job. It's an ugly fact, but it is true.

The sooner your loved one learns this, the quicker he or she will find a job. One of the most valuable skills in the job search is the ability to present oneself effectively to an employer. Most employers want people who are hard working, reliable, and able get the job done in a way that reflects positively on the company and its employees. Unfortunately, most job seekers only get a few minutes of face-to-face time to make that impression with employers. And during those few minutes, there must be nothing about you that suggests to the interviewer that you are anything but a top-notch employee.

There are several elements to making an effective personal presentation to employers. I will list the following three here:

- Dress

- Communication

- Mannerisms

Dress
Consider the following scenario, which actually happened:
It is a warm day in July, and a well-spoken gentleman, who had just been released from prison days earlier, walks into the office of a janitorial company after having been called for an interview. He is wearing cut-off jeans and a T-shirt that reek of cigarette smoke, with old, worn sneakers. He has spent the last four years of his life buffing floors, swilling toilets, and scrubbing sinks at the prison — activities which would make him qualified for the janitorial position he is seeking. The interview starts at 9:00 a.m. — he is there by 8:50 a.m. He is invited into the interviewer's office for an interview.

At 9:30 a.m., the first gentleman exits the interview, and another gentleman walks in. He is just as qualified and well-spoken as the first gentlemen, and he, too, has done janitorial work in prison. He is wearing a pair of neatly pressed khakis, brown soft-soled shoes, and a white button- down shirt. He has refrained from smoking cigarettes while dressed in his interview clothes, so that the cigarette smoke does not get onto his clothes.

Based on appearances alone, who do you think got the job?

While it would be a blessing to sit across the desk from an interviewer who can see beyond a person's clothing and external accouterments and focus on internal qualities, it usually does not work that way. Many employers have adopted the attitude of many in society today that suggests that the type of clothing you wear is a mirror of the type of person you are. Personally, I do not believe that is true. But that is the society that we live in. And in the few minutes that a potential employer has to judge whether or not you are the right person for the job, your clothing should be as conformist as possible.

I am not going to go into the type of clothing that should be worn at job interviews — there are plenty of good references on that subject. You are reading this book because you want to know how to help. The most important thing you can do is to see to it that your loved one has a good set of clothing to wear to job interviews and that he or she wears them. If your finances permit, purchase some clothing. If your finances do not permit, ask similarly sized friends if they have any extra clothing. I should stress that you are not looking for worn, tattered clothing. You are looking for clothing that is in relatively good shape. Any flaws in the clothes should be largely unnoticeable.

There may be outlet stores in your area that sell clothing at a bargain-basement price. Now, if you can afford to buy your loved one new clothes at regular clothing or department stores, then by all means, do it. But if I have to get clothes for an ex-offender, which I sometimes have to do on a limited budget, I usually go to places like Gabriel Brothers (check their web site at www.gabrielbrothers.com for locations), which sells good clothing at low prices. Some of the clothing may be slightly impaired (stains, tears, holes, mislabeled article size, etc.), so you really have to pay attention to what you buy. But largely, the damage on the clothing is so slight you would barely notice it, but the regular clothing stores can't sell it because it does not meet their definition of perfection.

Your loved ones do not have to go into the interview looking like they just stepped out of a GQ or Vanity Fair ad, but they should look clean and professional, wearing clothing appropriate to the atmosphere and type of job they are interviewing for.

Communication

Okay, so your loved one doesn't speak the King's English. Maybe your loved one has trouble putting two sentences together. There's nothing you will be able to do about that overnight, and the truth is, unless your loved one is interviewing for a job in which communication skills are important (such as telephone salespersons, writers, teachers, etc.), those things are not crucial. What is crucial is that your loved ones are able to clearly and effectively relay to the interviewer why they should be hired instead of the ten or twenty people waiting outside his door.

The best you can do here is to practice the art of interviewing with your loved one. If you do not consider yourself competent in that area, then try to find programs around town where your loved one can learn exactly what to say in a job interview and how to say it. And keep in mind that saying it involves more that just the lips and the voice. It involves the eyes, the ears, and, on occasion, the hands.

Your loved ones must be taught that when communicating with a person, they should make eye contact. (This is a skill that is beneficial beyond the realm of the interview.) They should listen for cues in the interviewer's voice that it is time to respond, or to comment, or to just shut up. Your loved one should be taught that his or her hands should remain in his or her lap, unless they are used to accentuate a point. Under no circumstances should your loved one do the following:

- Fidget.

- Look down or elsewhere during the interview.

- Appear eager to wrap up before the interview has finished.

- Use bad language, even if the interviewer uses it.

- Frown.

- Chew gum, eat, or drink during the interview, unless the interview offers something to drink. (Keep in mind that I have heard of an interviewer offering a potential employee something to drink, only to see how often he or she takes a sip of the drink. Frequent drinking often indicates nervousness and unease.)

- Interrupt the interviewer.

- Debate the interviewer. (It is permissible to politely disagree with a point the interviewer makes, as long as he knows *exactly* what he's talking about, and the issue is not too weighty. But if the interviewer persists in his point of view, leave it at that. He should try to stay away from giving his opinion about things, unless the interviewer asks.)

- Refuse to answer questions (except illegal ones).

- Stumble on answering questions.

How to answer when the interviewer asks about a gap in his employment history or asks about his incarceration

He should be honest. He should explain the situation and also explain how that situation has made him wiser, has helped him, or has made him a stronger person. He should never leave the interviewer with the impression that he is the same guy he was before he went to prison. If he lies about his incarceration history and is found out later (for instance, if a company hires pending a background check), he will lose his job. It is better to be honest up-front and risk not getting the job, than lie and get the job under false pretenses. He will never be entirely uncomfortable – – he will always be going through steps to make sure that he is not found out. Besides, many parole officers will call his job to verify his employment. If he has lied about going to prison, often the call from the parole officer will be enough to nail him.

Mannerisms
Understand that when an ex-offender is called in for an interview, the interviewer will typically pay as much attention to how he acts as to what he says. The one thing that will shoot him in the foot here is walking into an interviewer's office and acting like he's not the least bit interested in the job or acting like he does not care if he gets the job or not. When he is being interviewed, he should try to act like the job is interesting, even if it isn't. Bottom line: Many jobs that ex-offenders are eligible for upon release from prison are not jobs that they envisioned spending their whole lives doing. But remember, the goal is to get a job and work at it faithfully until a better one comes along. Proverbs 14:23 reminds us, "in all labor there is profit."

Reluctance of employers to hire ex-offenders
It is obviously true that there are many employers who will not hire ex-offenders. This practice may be illegal, depending on the state. [2] While this may make the job search difficult and trying at times, it is not impossible to find employers who will hire ex-offenders. What this means is that there must be diligence and patience in the job search. Whatever happens, encourage him NOT TO GIVE UP. If he works on presenting himself effec-

---

[2] Check with an attorney or with your state's labor department. Many have laws that bar discrimination against persons with an arrest or conviction record, unless the person is working or being considered for a job in which the circumstances of that job are closely tied to the circumstances of the crime(s). For instance, a person convicted of embezzlement or bank robbery probably will not be hired at a bank. A person arrested for or convicted of child molestation will not be allowed to work at a day care center, school, or any job involving contact with children.

tively and on being willing to work, a job will come along.

One issue here is that if an employer does not hire an ex-offender, it is commonly perceived to be because the applicant was an ex-offender. Often, there are other issues that contributed, such as no interest in the job or an inability to communicate effectively. Another issue is that it is easy to blame a failed job interview on the fact that the employer does not hire ex-offenders, which may not be the case.

I am reminded of the story of the beggar, who went to a busy intersection in the middle of rush hour to beg for change from cars that stopped at the red light. As the cars stopped for the light, he walked up the line of waiting cars, his hat in his hand, asking the drivers if they had any spare change. Most of the drivers said no and averted their gazes. In fact, the light changed four times, and not one person gave him a penny. This could have been enough of a discouragement to him to make him pack up and leave. But he stayed there until someone in the sixth group of cars reached his hand out of the window and dropped into the beggar's hat two crisp twenty-dollar bills. That one gift made all of the effort worthwhile. Had he given up, he would never have received that forty dollars.

There is a concept in marketing that goes like this: The more people you ask to buy your product, the more likely you are to sell it. Their goal is to get their product exposed to as many people as possible, because they know that not everyone will be interested in their product.

The bottom line is this: Patience, persistence, and diligence will get him a job. If an employer refuses to hire him, he should pack up and move on to the next employer. Every day he should make several job contacts. If he really wants to find a job, he should work eight hours a day on that task just as he would work eight hours once he finds the job. He should make *finding* a job his job!

Lack of desire to work

An employment counselor who works with our ministry once told me, "If they don't want to work, there's nothing you can do for them." There's no doubt that trying to get a slothful person to assume the responsibility of regular employment is like trying to get a pig to take regular bubble baths. As a result, "a lazy person has trouble all through life." [3]

Despite this, laziness has become popular. American culture is increasingly seeking to avoid work, rather than face it. Televisions, VCRs, microwaves, even the Internet have made us into a nation of sluggards and couch potatoes. There are a number of books on the market that give advice for those who consider themselves lazy. *The Lazy Person's Guide to Being Rich* and *The Lazy Person's Guide to Good Cooking* are a couple that I have heard of. I have even heard of seminars such as "Getting Rich in 30 Days," which cater to our desire to get something while putting as little work into it as possible.

Lazy ex-offenders not only will not work properly once they get a job, they will not put much effort into looking

---

[3] Proverbs 15:19

for one. I know ex-offenders here in the big city of Washington, DC, who tell me they have been looking for jobs for years without success. Now, maybe my naïveté is showing here, but how can anyone beat the streets for years, seriously and diligently looking for employment each day, several hours per day, in a major city, and not get anything? I believe that their job search was more similar to another ex-offender's job search. He confessed to me, while sitting in a jail cell because he violated his parole for not finding a job, that his job search consisted of hanging around the house, watching TV, checking the newspapers occasionally, and waiting for friends and relatives to inform him about job openings. He was on the streets about nine months and made about four job contacts in that entire time.

I disagree with the counselor's assessment that there is nothing you can do. In fact, there is. Laziness and slothfulness is directly related to lack of zeal and motivation. Seldom is a person lazy in everything he does. It is typical for a person to be lazy at one thing but very diligent and active in another. For instance, a child can be very active and involved in sports and outdoor activities but very lazy when it comes to studying. Another example is that many of us will put forth more effort in things that are perceived as "fun," than in things that we do not particularly like. I put forth a great deal of energy in writing this book, but don't ask me to do the dishes!

As a person trying to help a loved one who is or has been incarcerated, you will play a big role in helping to keep the ex-offender zealous and motivated.

What are the things that the ex-offender desires most in life? What were some of his dreams as a kid? What are his goals? It would be extremely helpful to find out what these things are and constantly remind him of these things and the work and effort he has to put forth to achieve them. Do not let him get deceived into thinking he can achieve these things without effort. The drugs lifestyle can lead him to believe that he can have everything he wants overnight. But with that lifestyle there is a price to pay—a price that could destroy all of his dreams and ambitions forever.

Most important, you, as a loved one, may be encouraging his laziness. If you are taking care of him, feeding him, providing a room over his head, buying him clothes, babysitting his kids, and letting him use your car, then he has no incentive whatsoever to do anything for himself. This is a dreadful mistake many loved ones make in the name of love! As long as he is being supported, he has no motivation to do anything.

A friend of mine recently told me about one of his coworkers. He mentioned that the coworker was lazy and didn't show up on time for work. Although he warned the coworker several times that his work ethic was horrible and encouraged him to do better, the coworker spent most of his days at work playing video games, taking cigarette breaks, and chit-chatting with other coworkers. My friend warned him again, even suggested that he could be fired, but the coworker never improved. Why? Because the coworker did not think he would get fired. He believed he was invincible.

Long story short, the coworker got fired. He walked out the door, still wondering why he got fired.

A lazy person will by nature get everyone else to do his work for him. If he can get his needs taken care of without lifting a finger, he will do so. And you are not helping him by continuing to cater to his needs.

God honors work. He desires that every man and woman pull their own weight, unless they are physically or mentally unable. Helping your loved ones break they couch-potato ways will lead them into greater self-sufficiency, not to mention making them happier because they can provide for themselves rather than relying on others. I remember when I had to beg and borrow in order to pay the rent. Now that I am more financially stable and able to care for myself, I am much more at peace. I don't have to wait for anyone to put food on the table. I can do it for myself. And there is even greater joy when I can do it for others until they are able to do it for themselves. I think one of the greatest expressions of love is when we can help others find their own way.

Medical problems

Some ex-offenders have medical problems that can hinder the type of employment they do or eliminate the possibility of employment altogether. If your loved one is unable to work because of a medical problem, he is considered disabled and may be eligible for federal government entitlements from the Social Security Administration. There are other perks available to those who are disabled, including reduced public transportation rates, subsidized rent, and free or reduced medical insurance (Medicaid, Medicare, etc.). If your loved one is disabled, I would strongly suggest you find a good, qualified agency in your area that works with the disabled. These agencies typically assign a caseworker who will work with your loved one through the period of disability and will refer him to appropriate services in the community. These agencies may be able to help your loved one apply for the Social Security Administration's disability insurance program, known as Supplemental Security Income (SSI) for the aged, blind, and disabled. Your state or city also may have a supplemental program of its own, which may be linked to the federal government program.

The federal government's definition of disability is pretty stringent. They will check your loved one's medical records thoroughly and may even have your loved one examined by one of their own doctors to confirm the disability. To be eligible, the medical condition must be so severe that it prevents the applicant from maintaining gainful employment regularly and consistently. Your loved one must have little-to-no income.

For more information, visit the Social Security Administration's web site at www.ssa.gov, or contact the local SSA office in your area.

Instead of disability, age, or blindness, your loved one may have medical problems that may not prevent him from working but will limit the type of work he can do and the jobs he can get. For instance, if he has respiratory problems, he might not be able to work in an environment where a lot of dust is generated, such as cleaning or excavation. If he has back problems, he may not be able to do heavy lifting. These factors make the job search more challenging, since it further limits the available pool of jobs that the ex-offender has to choose from. Again, such a situation may be difficult but not impossible.

Typically, the question on a job application that asks, "Do you have any medical problems that could hinder employment?" is asked to give the employer information to determine whether the job would be safe and healthy for the worker. However, it is also used to discriminate (i.e., against HIV-positive or AIDS patients who can work) and to weed out those applicants who the employer thinks will take a significant amount of time off the job due to illness.

It is best to steer clear of those jobs where the working environment could pose a danger to your loved one's health or welfare. If your loved one has medical problems, even minor ones, that could affect employment, researching jobs before applying is an absolute must. Find out all about the job before applying. I personally would not feel comfortable letting an employer make a determination as to whether I can work a job. Make sure you get enough information to make a determination on your own. And be aware—it is illegal for an employer to refuse to hire on the basis of a disability, unless that disability affects job performance.

Unavailability of adequate employment

Even after following all of the tips above, your loved one still may find it difficult to obtain employment, simply because there are not many options to choose from. If you live in or near a big city, this may not be as much of a problem. But if your loved one lives in a small town far away from a big city, or even in a big city where the job market is not favorable, a move to an area with a more bountiful job market may be in order. Again, this should be a last resort but is certainly worth considering if your loved one cannot find a job in his or her area.

Another option is to create a job. In other words, start a business. While the specifics of doing that are not within the scope of this book, it is certainly a feasible option if your loved one is enterprising enough to pull it off.

Starting a business is certainly not for someone who needs to reap immediate rewards for his labor, since most businesses do not turn a profit right away. It is also not for someone who does not have the resources to invest in equipment, personnel, training, facilities, and whatever else is required to get the business going.

But I would be remiss not to mention that many ex-offenders have decided to start their own businesses and have been successful. In fact, a few of the skills that some of them used to sell drugs and to run drug enterprises were used in legitimate businesses. While I certainly do not support or condone drug dealing, it remains one of the most lucrative businesses in the United States. To run a drug enterprise successfully requires a genius and business savvy that can be put to good use in lawful professions. Running a business would certainly be a viable option if your loved one can discover an unmet need and set about meeting that need.

In Washington, DC, there are dozens of ex-offenders making their living this way. Cleaning, moving and hauling, yard work, and auto maintenance are just a few of the endeavors they have engaged in. Many of these businesses require very little to get started and involve little personal cost. Some of these businesses are "under the table" and not registered with any authorities (which is not necessarily illegal), and many have shoddy business practices. Nonetheless, I applaud these efforts, since they are not dealing drugs or sitting around the house waiting for a big opportunity to fall from the sky.

A good source for information about starting a business can be found at the Small Business Administration (www.sba.gov). However, one of the major limitations with the SBA is that it does not accept applications for business loans from persons (or firm principals) who are incarcerated or on parole or on probation. However, the SBA web site has enough information to make it helpful despite that restriction.

CHAPTER THIRTEEN

Issues Concerning Women Ex-Offenders

The incarceration of women in this country is on the rise. The increase in the number of women in prison has outpaced the increase in the number of men since 1995. Since 1995, the number of female inmates has increased by 50 percent.

Table 4. Prisoners under the jurisdiction of State or Federal correctional authorities, by gender, 1995, 2003, and 2004

	Men	Women
All inmates		
6/30/04	1,390,906	103,310
6/30/03	1,363,813	100,384
12/31/95	1,057,406	68,468
Percent change, 2003-2004	2.0%	2.9%
Average annual, 1995-2004	3.3%	5.0%
Sentenced to more than 1 year		
6/30/04	1,333,791	94,192
6/30/03	1,308,891	91,245
12/31/95	1,021,059	63,963
Incarceration rate*		
6/30/04	923	63
6/30/03	915	62
12/31/95	789	47

*The total number of prisoners with a sentence of more than 1 year per 100,000 U.S. residents.

If your loved one is female, there are additional issues that you have to be aware of. In this chapter, we will deal with two issues, namely pregnancy and a female ex-offender's view of men.

View of men

Many women in prison today have a negative, distorted, or unhealthy view of men. Why? Many of them blame men for their problems. In many cases, it was a man who introduced them to drugs. In many cases, it was a man who abandoned the family and left the mother and her child to fend for themselves, leading to theft and robbery. In many cases, it was a man who sexually abused them, violating their trust and causing trauma that would lead to criminal behavior. In many cases, it was a man who intimidated them and made them do immoral and illegal things to win his love and respect. In many cases, it was serving the sexual needs of a man that lead them to be arrested and imprisoned.

Our ministry works closely with two halfway homes in the city that care for women offenders. These women are both pre-trial offenders and sentenced offenders. I have sat in on meetings and watched these women several times. While some men have had some level of success in dealing with these women, they overwhelmingly respond more to females than to males. This can be attributed to simple female camaraderie, but I think it is more. Two things that all of these women have in common are that they were arrested and that they were all dogged and mistreated by men.

"You don't need a man to complete you, to make you feel good about yourself," a woman told them in one such meeting. She is the director of a non-profit organization that reaches out to women in prison and halfway homes. Many of the stories she tells proclaim the power and independence of women and downplay the influence of men. The women respond favorably to these stories—the storyteller speaks their language, knows their pain and sorrows. She is an icon for them, probably because she understands first-hand where they come from.

A male minister and I tried to go into the halfway home to do ministry a few times, but it seemed as if we couldn't get through. The women looked at us with the caution and sense of danger of a child standing in the midst of scary strangers.

In dealing with female ex-offenders, you may encounter their distrust of men. Oftentimes this view is distorted and unhealthy and can cause problems for female ex-offenders coming into the community. Oftentimes this view is caused by years of experiences of men using them, abusing them, and treating them like they were lower than the things that crawl at night. Some women even go as far as to call men "dogs."

If your loved one is a woman, she may have these views, whether they are openly expressed or kept quiet. As such, it will affect her relationships with male supervisors, male pastors, and male members of her family, including her husband or boyfriend. This is not a problem that will necessarily result in her going back to prison, but it could affect her ability to relate to men in her life, which can only make re-entry more difficult. In this situation, unless you are a skilled counselor, it is best to pray for your loved one and try to get her to acknowledge she has a problem and get her to agree to undergo some counseling. Continue to reinforce the fact that her problem is not with the male sex, but with a few males in her life who have mistreated her. But do not blow this problem out of proportion. There are many women who distrust men, yet they are able to continue to relate to them and function normally in society.

Dealing with pregnant ex-offenders

The fact that your loved one is pregnant may complicate the process of getting her successfully reintegrated into society. A pregnancy will almost certainly affect the types of jobs she is able to perform, as well as the types of jobs she is able to accept. Therefore it is important to understand the job's maternity leave policy. Larger companies are covered by the Family and Medical Leave Act of 1993, which guarantees an expectant mother 12 weeks of unpaid leave. Following is a summary of this act:

1) Understand that the Family and Medical Leave Act of 1993 guarantees a new mother up to 12 weeks of unpaid leave if the company has more than 50 employees for at least 20 weeks of the year. The employee seeking the leave has to have been with the company at least one year.

2) Know that you can also use some of this time during your pregnancy, since it qualifies as a serious medical condition and is covered under the act.

3) Realize that your employer must keep your job, or one that is equivalent (in duties, pay, etc.), open for your return.

4) Recognize that your employer must continue your health insurance without charge while you

are gone. If you do not return to work, then you would have to reimburse your employer for the expense.

5) Give notice to your employer at least 30 days before you plan to take the time off. If an emergency develops, such as premature labor, give notice as soon as you can.

6) Do understand that your employer can require you to use up your paid leave first.

7) Take your 12 weeks in any blocks of time you like. You could decide to take 6 straight weeks and then every Tuesday and Thursday until you use up your time.

8) Look for a notice posted in your place of employment about your rights. This notice must be posted, or your employer is subject to fines.

9) Talk to your employer if you work for a company with fewer than 50 employees. Find out what the maternity leave policy is. Most employers offer at least 6 weeks unpaid leave.

10) Understand that the baby's father can also take a paternity leave with the same conditions as your maternity leave.

Preparations will also need to be made to welcome the little one upon arrival, as well as arrange for childcare.

Another issue regarding pregnancy that could certainly complicate matters involves the mother's motivation for getting pregnant. Social workers all over the country have encountered the type of woman who, because she cannot or is unwilling to find a job or a man to take care of her, will get pregnant. Immediately after the child is born, she will apply for welfare assistance from the federal government, called Temporary Aid to Needy Families (TANF). As appalling as this sounds, many women know that they are guaranteed to get some type of assistance if they have a child.

In my opinion, only a lazy, shiftless woman would do such a thing. The majority of mothers in this country love their children and would work two, three, sometimes four jobs to provide for them. But unfortunately, there are those for whom children is only a fiscal convenience.

If you sense that your loved one is this way, then by all means try to convince her to get some counseling. She is living dangerously whenever she gets pregnant or uses her child to get money and resources for herself. Let her know that under the current TANF regulations, she must find a job or enroll in job training within a certain period of time because the benefits are only temporary. Eventually she will need to find a job. She might as well find one now, rather than waiting until the public dole runs out.

A woman who has this mentality may also seek out men primarily for fiscal benefits. Be aware of this and watch your loved one's relationships with men closely. If she truly loves and appreciates the man in her life, that is one thing. But if she seems to be using the man for what she can get out of him, that is a sign of danger. She is almost assuredly on a path back to prison, because she does not recognize the need to take care of her own responsibilities and stop depending on the government or men to do it for her. A woman like this is not far from stealing, and she may eventually move in that direction if her behavior is not checked as soon as possible.

Appendix

National Agencies That May Be of Assistance to Those Helping Inmates and Ex-offenders

Prison Fellowship Ministries
44180 Riverside Parkway
Lansdowne, VA 20176-8421
1-800-478-0100
www.pfm.org
An international family of ministries founded in 1976 by former Nixon aide Chuck Colson. Prison Fellowship has several ministries that work with inmates, ex-offenders, families of offenders, and crime victims. Its family-of-ex-offender-oriented ministries includes Angel Tree, which provides gifts to children of prisoners at Christmas and has expanded to helping churches mentor Angels and send them to summer camp.

Citizens United for Rehabilitation of Errants (CURE National)
P.O. Box 2310
Washington, DC 20013-2310
202-789-2126
www.curenational.org
CURE is a non-profit, nationwide organization dedicated to the reduction of crime through the reform of the criminal justice system. They are a prison and jail reform advocacy group headquartered in Washington, DC, with chapters or affiliates in most states. Among the changes they seek are fair and humane treatment for prisoners, far less reliance on incarcera-

tion as a solution to crime problems, far more reliance on alternatives to prisons, and the abolishment of capitol punishment.

Family and Corrections Network (FCNETWORK)
32 Oak Grove Road
Palmyra, VA 22963-2534
434-589-3036
www.fcnetwork.org
FCNetwork is for and about the families of offenders. They offer information on children of prisoners, parenting programs for prisoners, prison visiting, incarcerated fathers and mothers, hospitality programs, how to keep in touch, return to the community, the impact of the justice system on families, and prison marriage. With over 100,000 visitors a year, this web site is an excellent gateway to policy, and research on families of offenders.

America's Second Harvest
35 E. Wacker Dr., Suite 2000
Chicago, IL 60601-2200
1-800-771-2303
312-263-2303
www.secondharvest.org
America's Second Harvest is the nation's largest domestic hunger-relief organization. Through a network of over 200 food banks and food-rescue programs, they distribute food to 26 million hungry Americans each year, eight million of whom are children.

The Food Stamp Program (US Department of Agriculture)
1-800-221-5689
www.fns.usda.gov
The Food Stamp Program helped put food on the table for some 7.3 million households and 17.2 million individuals each day in Fiscal Year 2000. It provides low-income house-

holds with coupons or electronic benefits they can use like cash at most grocery stores to ensure that they have access to a healthy diet. The Food Stamp Program is the cornerstone of the federal food assistance programs, and provides crucial support to needy households and to those making the transition from welfare to work. It provided an average of $1.25 billion a month in benefits in Fiscal Year 2000.

The US Department of Agriculture (USDA) administers the Food Stamp Program at the federal level through its Food and Nutrition Service (FNS). State agencies administer the program at state and local levels, including determining eligibility and allotments and distributing benefits.

Local food stamp offices can provide information about eligibility, and the USDA operates a toll-free number (800-221-5689) for people to receive information about the Food Stamp Program. For more information about the Food Stamp Program or any of the Food and Nutrition Service's 15 nutrition assistance programs, contact the Food and Nutrition Service Communications Staff at 703-305-2281, or by mail at 3101 Park Center Drive, Alexandria, Virginia 22302-1500. You can also e-mail them at FSPHQ-WEB@fns.usda.gov.

National Association of Alcohol and Drug Addiction Counselors (NAADAC)
901 N. Washington Street, Suite 600
Alexandria, VA 22314-1535
1-800-548-0497
703-741-7686
www.naadac.org.
The NAADAC's mission is to lead, unify, and empower addiction-focused professionals to achieve excellence through education, advocacy, knowledge, standards of practice, ethics, professional development, and research.

References

Beckner, Dr. W. Thomas and Jeff Park, ed., *Effective Jail and Prison Ministry for the 21st Century*. Charlotte, NC: Coalition of Prison Evangelists, 1998. Available from www.copeministries.org

Bolles, Richard Nelson and Mark Emery Bolles. *What Color is your Parachute? 2005: A Practical Manual for Job-Hunters and Career-Changers*. Berkeley, CA: Ten Speed Press, 2005. This book is updated each year and may be ordered from www.amazon.com or through your local bookstore.

The National Legal Aid and Defender Association. *The Directory of Legal Aid and Defender Offices in the United States and Territories*. Washington, DC: The National Legal Aid and Defender Association, 2004. This directory is published biannually. To order, contact the National Legal Aid and Defender Association, 1625 K Street, NW, Suite 800, Washington, DC 20006-1604 or online at www.nlada.org.

Jones, Louis N. *I Need A J-O-B! The Ex-Offender's Job Search Manual*. Washington, DC. Conquest Publications, 2005. Available from www.conquesthouse.org.

Smarto, Donald. *Keeping Ex-Offenders Free! An Aftercare Guide*. Grand Rapids, MI: Baker Pub Group, 1994. Available from www.amazon.com or through your local bookstore.

Stewart, Marcia, Janet Portman, and Ralph Warner. *Every Landlord's Legal Guide*. 7th ed. Nolo.com: October 2004. Available for download online from www.amazon.com in PDF format.

Wright, Lois and Cynthia B. Seymour. *Working with Children and Families Separated by Incarceration..* Washington,

DC: CWLA Press, 2000. To order, contact Child Welfare League of America, 440 First Street, NW, Third Floor, Washington, DC 20001-2085